Good Cook's Book *of* Mustard

Other Books by Michele Anna Jordan

More Than Meatballs

Vinaigrettes & Other Dressings

The World Is a Kitchen

Lotsa Pasta

VegOut! A Guide Book to Vegetarian Friendly Restaurants in Northern California

The BLT Cookbook

San Francisco Seafood

The New Cook's Tour of Sonoma

Pasta Classics

California Home Cooking

Polenta

Pasta with Sauces

Ravioli & Lasagne

The Good Cook's Journal

The Good Cook's Book of Tomatoes

The Good Cook's Book of Salt & Pepper

The Good Cook's Book of Oil & Vinegar

A Cook's Tour of Sonoma

The
Good Cook's Book
of Mustard

ONE OF THE WORLD'S MOST BELOVED
CONDIMENTS, WITH MORE THAN 100 RECIPES

MICHELE ANNA JORDAN

PHOTOGRAPHY BY LIZA GERSHMAN

FOREWORD BY MADELEINE KAMMAN

Skyhorse Publishing

Skyhorse Publishing books may be purchased in bulk at special discounts for
sales promotion, corporate gifts, fund-raising, or educational purposes. Special
editions can also be created to specifications. For details, contact the Special Sales
Department, Skyhorse Publishing, 307 West 36th Street, 11th Floor, New York, NY
10018 or info@skyhorsepublishing.com.

Skyhorse® and Skyhorse Publishing® are registered trademarks of Skyhorse
Publishing, Inc.®, a Delaware corporation.

Visit our website at www.skyhorsepublishing.com.

10 9 8 7 6 5 4 3 2 1

Library of Congress Cataloging-in-Publication Data is available on file.

Cover design by Erin Seaward-Hiatte
Cover photo credit: Liza Gershman

Print ISBN: 978-1-63220-586-5
Ebook ISBN: 978-1-63450-013-5

Printed in China

In memory of my friend Mary Frances Kennedy "MFK" Fisher

1908–1992

Contents

Part 4: Appendices

Foreword

We tend to take our food for granted because we have to eat. So, we often eat without ever giving thanks to whichever deity we worship for our daily fare. Or then, tipping the scale way down in the opposite direction, some of us look at food, not as deserving of our full gratitude or to be enjoyed unconditionally, but as a part of a strict social rite to practice with business partners, or even, in extreme cases, as a way to climb the ladder of fame.

Mercifully there are also the others, all those who work in small communities, keeping the flame of good fare burning for all, using their fresh local ingredients with enthusiasm and personal flair, teaching the gospel of purity and simplicity. Michele Jordan is one of these dedicated souls. Long before she came to the School for American Chefs as my student, I noticed her well-written articles in a Sonoma County newspaper and admired her good culinary sense and techniques.

Michele has now written a very lively book on the liveliest of all condiments and my very favorite of all: the lowly mustard. May this attractive volume bring all cooks and inveterate cookbook readers a joyous renewed acquaintance with this oldest and most popular taste booster.

Madeleine Kamman
Director and Professor
School of American Chefs, Beringer Vineyards
St. Helena, CA, October 1993

Acknowledgments

I would like to take this opportunity to publicly apologize to Barry Levenson, founder of the Mt. Horeb Mustard Museum and curator of the National Mustard Museum: Barry, I am truly sorry for referring to you as Barry Lawrence back in 1996 when you were on my radio show, *Mouthful*. It is one of the things that haunts me at 3 a.m. when I can't sleep. Please chalk it up to my novice days as a radio host, when I was nervous and occasionally misspoke, over and over. And thank you for your ongoing passion for all things mustard; you've added a coat of bright yellow to the world.

And thanks to Kermit Lynch Wine Merchant for carrying *PIC* Dijon mustard; it is one of my all-time favorites and you've saved me thousands in air fare to the South of France. Dammit.

Once again, I am indebted to Nicole Frail and the team at Skyhorse Publishing for making this a fulfilling project despite or perhaps because of the crazy schedule. *Y'all are great!* I offer a special shout-out to the design team for listening to my reservations and coming up with such a great cover design.

Liza Gershman's photographs in this book are spectacular. *Thank you so much, Liza.* And thank you, Rayne "Prop Mistress" Wolfe for your dedication and inspiration with styling. Big thanks, as well, to Nancy Lorenz, Kelly Keagy, my grandson Lucas and everyone else who helped with the photo sessions. And to my neighbors, Amy, Leslie and Kelsey, thank you for not minding that I stole your ladder a couple of times. I wish you much happiness in your new home but am very sad you've moved away from out sweet little hilltop.

Speaking of sweet little hilltops, I am deeply indebted to the wonderful Mary Duryee for the lovely home where I have lived for almost, gulp, thirty years. I knew the moment I saw the little high-ceilinged south-facing room that my Muse would be happy in the space and indeed she is. Together, we are still going strong. *Mary, thank you, from the deepest recesses of my heart and soul.*

I send a big *merci beaucoup* to Joanne Derbort, my editor at the *Santa Rosa Press Democrat* and *Sonoma* magazine, for being the essential cog in the crazy machine of my writing life. And to the entire newspaper and magazine teams, *thank you thank you thank you.*

Special thanks, again, to Clark Wolf, for wisdom, support, passion and encouragement.

And to Ken Behrens, thanks for all your help with all things electronic, all things wood, all things mechanical and and and . . . you're a great friend and I deeply appreciate all you do for us.

And to my closest friends and family, especially James Carroll and John Boland, my daughter Nicolle and her husband Tom, my daughter Gina and her extraordinary son Lucas, thank you again, for absolutely everything.

And now, let's eat! Please pass the mustard . . .

Introduction
to the Second Edition

So much has changed in the world of food since I began writing The Good Cook's series in the early 1990s, with a single exception: Mustard.

Interest in one of the world's favorite condiments has increased, with mustard festivals, including the Napa Valley Mustard Festival, launched the year after The Good Cook's Book of Mustard was published, and both local and national mustard competitions. Barely a year passes that I don't get a home-crafted mustard in the mail.

It's mustard itself that has not changed. The major styles—Dijon, coarse-grain, English, and American ballpark mustard among them—remain what they have been for decades and in some cases, centuries.

There are scores of new flavored mustards, too, mustards with chocolate nibs, cranberries, raspberries, chipotles, lavender, blue cheese, figs, all manner of herbs, and more. About the only type of mustard I've never seen is licorice, and I expect it to appear sometime soon.

Yet mustard itself endures, just as it is, without the discovery of heritage varieties or the development of new hybrids. Mustard is mustard, perfect as it has been for millennia, and that is a good thing.

So, what has changed since I wrote the first edition of this book, and what does it offer that the first edition doesn't?

I have changed, matured as a cook, grown in confidence as a writer, found both my footing and my voice. I look back on the original manuscript and, honestly, I am proud of it, especially of the research I did at a time when the Internet was not much more than a glimmer in a few pairs of eyes. I spent time in libraries, relied on research librarians, reached

out via snail mail, and traveled to France as I sought the story of mustard. I have left the narrative section of the book much as it was.

The recipes are almost completely new, except for the chapter of homemade mustards, as basic recipes and techniques have not changed at all. Other recipes reflect my travels since that first edition, my constant experimenting in the kitchen, my developing skills, and our ability to communicate world-wide in an instant.

One other thing has not changed, and that is the vitality of the mustard seed. It still spreads over the landscape like a bright yellow fever, a spring fever that announces the changing season. It is especially riveting when you are drunk with love, traveling down a back road, marveling in its golden beauty and thinking of your sweetie.

Introduction
to the First Edition

In March of 1993, I was on the train headed north from New York City to Saratoga Springs, and from there to Yaddo, the artists' colony on the outskirts of town. A few days earlier, I had left California's Sonoma County in the full bud of spring, its greens and golds and yellows stretched out over the countryside that I had loved and thrived in for over two decades. As I rode through the stark gray Hudson River Valley, the earth was wrapped in a monotone dream, nothing but the soft, uniform colors of winter in the Northeast, a sight entirely new to this born-and-bred California girl. The journey became a barren dreamscape between youthful California and the enduring splendor of Yaddo, a magical piece of land already alive with creative energy when my homeland was still in the early struggles of new statehood. In 1849, a year before California became a state, Edgar Allan Poe composed *The Raven* on the site that was to become Yaddo. What a profound joy it was to walk where he walked, to see what he saw. Yaddo has changed little since those years.

For two months, I would neither cook nor test a recipe nor wander through gourmet shops looking for inspiration among the wines and the oils, the vinegars and the honeys, the mustards. I would not visit a farmers market, nor would I gather armfuls of wild spring mustard for my table. Rather, I would spend my days and nights writing and reading and reflecting in the protected solitude that only an artists' colony can provide. I would work on a project about my friend and mentor, M. F. K. Fisher. As I anticipated the weeks ahead, and of time spent immersing myself in her work and of mingling my voice with hers, I thought of some of our last days together and of a particular visit nearly a year earlier, in the last spring of her life.

In that spring of 1992, California was in its sixth year of drought. January was dry; February brought no rain; in March each day was bright and harsh. Thirst prevailed in all of us and in everything: in the fields and hills that were the dry gold of summer already, in the deer who came down toward the towns and cities to find food and water, in the streams and creeks that had slowed to a trickle or less. We were very thirsty. And then in early April, the rains at last came, glorious torrents that drenched the thirsty soil, germinating seeds that had long lain dormant. The rains were not enough to ease the drought; those would come the next year. But they were sufficient to awaken the sleeping mustard, a hearty seed that can drowse within the soil for a hundred years, awaiting the proper conditions.

The mustard that bloomed soon after was the most beautiful, most abundant any of us had seen in years, perhaps decades. Every piece of undeveloped land seemed covered in a bright yellow fever. Mustard was woven between grapevines like gold stitches on a patchwork quilt; it stretched over the vast open spaces between the towns and cities of Sonoma County; it covered the low, lush hills of Alexander Valley in a profusion of golden blossoms. The hearty yellow flowers pushed through cracks in sidewalks and cement. It was a glorious, dizzying display, and it was through this golden turmoil that I drove to see my friend.

With her vocal cords ravaged by illness, Mary Frances could no longer converse, so during my visits, I often read to her. To capture the spirit of this warm day with its mustard covering the hills around us, I had brought along a story I had written called "Mustard Love," about my first spring in Sonoma County, when I lived in the low hills east of the town of Petaluma in an area known as Lakeville and drove daily through the back roads to the university where I was a student. There were no housing developments in Lakeville at that time, no shopping centers or luxury homes; there was, in fact, nothing much at all except eucalyptus trees and sweeping, gilded fields of mustard, nearly heartbreaking in their beauty. It reminded me of a train ride between Paris and Epernay, where for mile after mile as far as the eye could see there had been nothing but golden mustard and the sharp blue sky.

Mary Frances apparently enjoyed the piece, smiling and shrugging her shoulders in a characteristically evocative gesture that always seemed to convey pleasure. We talked of Dijon, and of the intriguing black facade of the Grey Poupon store on the corner of rue de la Liberté where we had both bought mustard. After our visit, as I wound my way back through the yellow hills to my home in Sebastopol, *The Good Cook's Book of Mustard* sprung to mind, fully formed and in clear focus. Once its publication was secured, I told Mary Frances of the project, of how I conceived of it that day with her when we read the mustard story, of how together we had evoked so vividly my memories of France in the spring and the tastes and smells of Dijon. The book was clearly hers, I said, as the dedication would show. Beyond words at all by that time, she gripped my hand, hunched up her shoulders, and beamed for a minute. I felt she approved and was pleased, even though she often criticized single-subject cookbooks. I kissed her hand and, for the first time in her presence, had to hold back tears. She died just a few days later, on June 22, 1992. I hope this book tells a story that would make her proud to appear on its first pages.

Although this book began as both a simple labor of love and an exploration of a favorite ingredient, it quickly became an exercise in fun and good humor as well. There is something about mustard that makes people act, well, silly. During the year or so that I worked on the manuscript, I came across inane recipes, goofy T-shirts, buttons shouting "Please Pass the Mustard," and even a silent film from the 1920s complete with a mock trial of a gentleman ignorant enough to try to eat a ham sandwich without mustard. The sandwich, represented by a skilled and wonderfully costumed actor, offered crucial evidence. Before too long, my trail led me to the court jester of mustard humor, Barry Levenson, and his Mount Horeb Mustard Museum in Mount Horeb, Wisconsin.

The discovery of Barry and his passion was like tapping into a great golden vein of subterranean mustard. Barry loves mustard, collects it, writes about it, and sells it. He epitomizes the lighthearted exuberance, the robust silliness, and expansive good humor with which mustard lovers pursue their hearts' desire.

Barry's food emporium offers scores of commercial mustards that I have not seen elsewhere. I decided to try a selection of his favorites. The box arrived by second-day air and I set out with every intention of being judicious and measured in my tasting, trying three or four, writing for a while, sampling again, so that my palate would be fresh and open for each new round. About thirty minutes later, I was happily lost in a golden fog, dozens of mustard jars open around me, spoons everywhere, all of my mineral water gone, cracker crumbs scattered like confetti testifying to my frenzied feast. One particular jar sat empty, a Vidalia onion mustard that is without doubt the best commercial mustard condiment I have ever tasted. I took a deep breath and settled back to recover.

Mustard at its best is like that, conducive of harmless indulgence and lusty good times. It is with this spirit that I suggest you approach finding your favorite mustard condiments, with enthusiasm informed by the hints and guidelines I offer throughout this book. I wish you as much of a good time as I had, and as I continue to have as new mustards appear on the market almost weekly.

Finally, I couldn't possibly write about one of my favorite foods without allowing myself to indulge in touting my specific preferences. This is not an objective assessment, but rather a highly opinionated tribute to the mustards I like best of all. *The Good Cook's Book of Mustard* is not really about commercial mustards or about condiments made with the spice. It is about mustard itself, its many varieties and preparations, its history and early uses, the folklore that attributes specific powers to it, and the many ways it functions in the kitchen. Still, when we cook with mustard, we must choose from among the hundreds that line our market shelves. I'm happy to share the ones that I prefer.

My favorite brand of mustard is a sassy little Dijon from the French company PIC, imported exclusively by a store in Berkeley, California, Kermit Lynch Wine Merchant, which also imports some of Italy's finest olive oils and great French and Italian wines. The mustard is irresistibly good and I'm forever sneaking fingerfuls of it as I walk past one of several mustard shelves in my kitchen. I like it so much I buy it by the case. When making, say, mustard cream, I notice a significant difference when I use PIC. It is the most suave, elegant mustard I have come across. After PIC, I favor Dessaux and L'Etoile for Dijon mustards, and when I can't find those, Grey Poupon serves me well. I often hear Grey Poupon Dijon mustard, now made domestically by Nabisco Foods, Inc., criticized and I heartily disagree. Licensed by Grey Poupon of France to produce the only Dijon mustard outside of France, Nabisco does an outstanding job. The texture is perfect and if it's not quite as strong as the French-made Grey Poupon, it still packs a good wallop of heat. The flavors are well balanced, and it is not overly salty. Grey Poupon is one of the few excellent ingredients that one can find in nearly every supermarket. And it is relatively inexpensive, so don't break your budget looking for the most exotic Dijon mustard around. Good Dijon mustard from French producers is often a treat, and I pick up new ones when I see them. But for day-to-day cooking, when I need mustard for a sauce or a soup, I know that l will get consistently good, reliable flavor with Grey Poupon. Maille, a French company older than Grey Poupon, makes an excellent Dijon, as well as a green peppercorn mustard that has a superb flavor, although I don't like that it contains vegetable oil, an unnecessary addition.

I don't care for most of the Dijon-style mustards made in this country, either by major companies or by small producers. I wish I could say otherwise, but I can't. I find they have a floury texture and lack both the compelling flavor of my favorites and the elegant texture of the French mustards. There are, however, scores of wonderful flavored mustards made by small companies all over the country, many of which begin with a commercial mustard base that is most often imported. I am wild about the Vidalia onion mustard made by Oak Hill Farms in Atlanta, Georgia; Duck Puddle Farm of Ivyland, Pennsylvania, makes a fine Southwestern mesquite mustard that is great with smoked poultry (or by the spoonful). A lovely whole-grain mustard is made by Arran Provisions on the Isle of Arran, Scotland; and l love the dark richness of the black mustard made by Wilson's of Essex, England.

And finally, a hot dog on the street in New York City, San Francisco, Santa Rosa, anywhere at all, should be topped with any humble ballpark mustard, sharp and bright and perfectly suited to its purpose.

PART I
All About Mustard

What is Mustard?

A friend opens his desk drawer and there sits a tiny plastic package, one side white, the other clear, revealing the bright yellow mixture inside: Ballpark or American mustard, a remnant of a now forgotten lunch on the run, a sandwich at his desk, perhaps, or egg rolls from the nearby Thai restaurant, which are always accompanied by the little packets. This is a scene repeated across the country daily, people finding little packages of mustard when they open their desk drawers, their cars' glove compartments, the packets of silverware and condiments on airlines, a bag holding a deli sandwich or some Chinese-to-go. Millions of little packages of mustard spurt their yellow interiors each year; millions more are discarded, forgotten, tossed into the corner of the pantry. Ask an American child about mustard and chances are the description will closely resemble the sharp yellow paste inside the little packet my friend found. This is mustard as most Americans have known it in this century, the mustard M. F. K. Fisher described as tasting "bright yellow," a flavor she considered essential to her chilled buttermilk soup. It is, indeed, our mustard, but it is not mustard as most of the world has known it or knows it today.

Mustard is a plant, a member of the Brassica genus of the Cruciferae family, so named for its flowers, which sport four petals in a cross-like configuration. All varieties of mustard are fast growing and, like other brassicas, thrive in cooler weather. Mustard blooms in the early spring and, in many areas, its bright yellow flowers are the first sign of the coming of the new season. Each mustard plant produces hundreds of seeds that are grouped together in pods. Today, commercial mustard seed comes from

just three species of Brassica, but the seeds of mustard plants, both wild and cultivated, have been used for millennia to season the foods we eat. In earliest times, the seeds were chewed with meat, possibly to disguise the flavor of decay. There are records of mustard's cultivation as early as 5000 to 4000 B.C., and mustard seeds have been found in Egypt's great pyramids. In A.D. 42, Columella's *De Re Rustica* included a recipe similar to today's well-known mustard sauce, which is simply a mixture of ground mustard seed, acidic liquid, and seasonings. Although technically, mustard can refer to the entire plant, it is prepared mustard, this sauce with such ancient roots, that we think of when we hear the word. What is it, exactly, that has intrigued the human palate for so many thousands of years?

The characteristic quality of mustard is its sharp, bright heat, an element that is released partially by the simple chewing of the raw seed. This sensation is the result of a chemical reaction that occurs when the outer shell, or husk, of the mustard seed is shattered and its cellular structure broken. The enzyme myrosin, in the presence of oxygen and water, reacts with a glucoside within the seed's heart to produce a particularly volatile substance, acrinyl isothiocyanate in white mustard, and allyl isothiocyanate in brown and black mustards. With white mustard, the burning sensation caused by this compound is felt only on the tongue. With brown and black mustards, there is also a sense of vaporization that affects the eyes, nose, and sinuses in much the same way as with Japanese wasabi. This sensation is activated by the same chemical, the glucoside sinigrin. The reaction is both the key to mustard's intrigue and the reason mustard was not widely accepted in the United States until 1904, when Francis French developed a mild recipe based exclusively on white mustard seeds. He suspected that Americans were not buying mustard because they did not like its heat, and his success suggests that he was right. Today, French's mustard—bright yellow from turmeric and tart from vinegar—accounts for 40 percent of all mustard consumed in this country. The rest of the world, however,

seems to prefer mustard not only with more heat, but also with more nuance and range of flavor.

Mustard's many nuances come not so much from its natural flavors, but from the ingredients used to produce the paste or sauce. There is limited variation in mustard itself: mild and hot, and coarse-ground or smooth. It is the choice of liquids, of flavoring agents, and the degree of milling that determines the subtle variations in a particular mustard's taste and texture. A variety of liquids—from apple cider vinegar and lemon juice to wine and beer—may contribute their flavors, and a broad range of herbs, spices, and aromatics add essential elements. Nearly all mustards are, and should be, finished with the addition of salt, which not only helps preserve the flavors, but, because salt dissolves on the tongue, also brings them together in a harmonious finish on the palate.

Although it is mustard the sauce, the condiment, that we think of when we hear mustard, the word also refers to the dry ground seeds, many types of greens, and, in regional slang, to the delicious yellow fat in the center of a crab's body. What you receive when you ask for "the mustard" varies greatly with where you do the asking. Certainly, if you're standing at the elbow of a crab picker in Maryland, you just might get that delicious fat. In many regions of France, you would be given a pot of Dijon, though in certain areas you might receive a tart, coarse-grained mixture, the mustard of Bordeaux or of Meaux. In America's heartland and in diners nearly everywhere, you would receive a plastic squeeze bottle of the bright yellow sauce. In restaurants in cities like Berkeley, San Francisco, Boston, Chicago, and New York, however, you would receive a more fashionable mixture, probably a Dijon, but possibly a house-made specialty mustard. In delicatessens, your options might be limited to American brown mustard, a mildly spicy mustard that is less tart than ballpark mustard. In Chinese restaurants throughout North America, a small bowl of very hot mustard, a simple mix of water and hot mustard flour, would be set on your table. In Germany, the mixture might be coarse or smooth, but in either case it would probably be brown rather than yellow, somewhat sweet, and fairly hot. In England, it would depend on where you were, although in most places you probably wouldn't have to ask for mustard. It is automatically served with roast beef, bangers, Cheddar cheese, and other standard British fare. Many pubs feature their own house blends, and the English are known for their hot mustards.

Interestingly, mustard as a condiment seems to be most popular in northern temperate climates. It is not widely used in Latin America (although it is popular in Argentina, where beef is a major part of the diet) nor in most of Africa. The Arab world has largely ignored mustard. India uses mustard oil and mustard seed, but prepared mustard is not among the many condiments that accompany most Indian meals. With limited exceptions, mustard does not play a significant role in the cuisines of southern Europe either.

Cutting the Mustard

The phrase "cut the mustard" is a common contemporary expression, indicating that someone is up to the task or the standards at hand. According to the 1986 edition of The Dictionary of American Slang, it entered the English language in the early 1900s from Philadelphia, where it was said that "groups . . . have special vested interests. And that's not gonna cut the mustard." It is suggested that mustard refers to "the genuine thing" and may be based on mustard as hot, keen, and sharp, all of which can also mean excellent.

The History of a Plant

An endless field of bright yellow mustard stretching as far as the eye can see is a glorious sight and one that is repeated throughout the world each spring. Mustard thrives in any temperate climate and requires no special care to grow. Rather the opposite, actually; so prolific and hardy is the

plant that it is often considered a weed. Mustard, however brilliant in the spring, is commonplace. Although it is the world's second most popular spice—only black pepper is consumed in greater quantity—no wars have been fought to obtain it and it has never commanded a high price on the world market.

Mustard, the plant, received its common name from the prepared condiment *mustum*, referring to the unsweetened, unfermented grape juice with which it was blended by the Romans, and *ardens*, referring to its fiery taste. Although just three species of the genus Brassica are harvested to produce what we generally call mustard, the word itself sometimes is used to indicate all brassicas, making such diverse vegetables as broccoli, cabbages, bok choy, Brussels sprouts, cauliflower, kale, kohlrabi, rutabaga, and turnip seem more closely related than they actually are. They are indeed part of the same family, Cruciferae, and of the same genus, Brassica, but they belong to different species entirely. All brassicas display the four-petaled flowers of their family, all are fast growing, and all flourish in cooler weather. Most members of the large group also contain chemicals that, in the presence of oxygen, precipitate a reaction that creates a volatile, irritating oil, but in many members, it is released primarily as an aroma rather than as a sensation on the palate. Only a few member plants produce the sort of heat given off by mustard.

Humans have taken advantage of mustard's savory qualities for thousands of years, and because its use extends far back into prehistory, it is impossible to know its exact origins with certainty. There are indications that mustard seeds were chewed by our ancestors as long as ten thousand years ago. These seeds would have been gathered from wild mustard. Records indicate that mustard was cultivated in China four or five thousand years before the birth of Christ. White mustard heralds from the eastern Mediterranean. Black mustard was first recorded in Persia, and brown mustard had its genesis in the Himalayan region, although the plant appears to have migrated to three separate regions—China, the southern

Ukraine, and the Indian subcontinent (India, Pakistan, and Bangladesh)—where it developed distinct and different characteristics. Although today the majority of mustard worldwide is made from the seeds of Brassica *juncea*, the variety that developed in Bangladesh was unsuitable for this purpose. Its seeds were—and are—used for their oil.

Romans took the mustard seed with them to Gaul, thus introducing what would become a spice strongly identified with France and French cuisine. Dijon, ancient capital of Burgundy in eastern France, today is considered the capital of the mustard world. Indeed, its very name is synonymous with the prepared condiment and over half of the world's prepared mustard comes from Dijon. From France, the use of mustard spread throughout Europe, into England, and to America with the first Spanish explorers. It grows wild throughout North America, although it is generally believed that Spanish *padres* scattered it along the Pacific Coast, where it flourishes today. Upon his return to America after serving as minister to France, Thomas Jefferson planted mustard in his garden and ordered the prepared condiment from Paris. Mustard naturalizes quickly—that is, it reseeds itself and needs no human intervention to thrive—and by the time of the Civil War, some seventy years after Jefferson's planting, there were plenty of greens from the wild mustard in the region to provide essential nourishment for the soldiers.

Today, mustard grows wild in every temperate region of the world. It is cultivated in many countries, but Canada supplies the majority of the world's commercial mustard needs. Additionally, commercial farmers and home gardeners grow dozens of types of mustards. It is a robust, fast-growing plant whose leaves make an excellent green for both salads and sautéing. Some varieties have a great deal of heat, even when they are quite young; others are milder, with just a hint of mustard's characteristic fire. Mustard sprouts also provide an interesting, easy way to introduce mustard's spicy flavor into our diets. They can be grown on any kitchen counter, and can be used whenever more common sprouts—alfalfa or

VARIETIES OF LEAF MUSTARD
Brassica Juncea

These mustards represent the nonhybrid seed currently available in the United States.

Variety	Other Names	Description
Aka Takana	India mustard	Large dark purple leaves with white ribs, pungent
Ao Takana	India mustard	Large bright green leaves, pungent
Common Leaved	Chinese Leaf mustard	Dwarf with thick stems
Curled	new in 1987	
Dai Gai Choi	Broadleaf Mustard Cabbage	Tall, large green leaves, broad stems, closed heads; mustard flavor
Florida Broad Leaf	Large Smooth Leaf	Round or oval serrated dark green leaves, cream-colored ribs
Florida Giant	new in 1991	
Fordhook Fancy	Burpee's Fordhook Fancy	Fringed deeply curled dark green leaves; mild
Gai Choi	Chinese Mustard Cabbage, Chinese Mustard Spinach, India mustard	Tall; mild but distinct mustard flavor
Giant Curled		Deep green leaves, crimped and frilled at edges; mild
Giant Curled Chinese	India mustard	Bright green curly leaves; excellent as cooked greens or in salads
Giant Red	Japanese mustard	Large deep purplish red leaves with white ribs; strong mustard flavor
Giant Southern Curled		Large bright green leaves, curled and fringed on edges
Green Wave	Yellow/Green Curly; Chinese Green Wave	Darkest green of curly mustards; spineless, deeply frilled; spicy hot flavor

onion, for example—are called for. They are particularly good on chicken sandwiches and on simple cream cheese sandwiches, where they add a bright spark of flavor.

Mustard's agricultural importance reaches beyond its use as a food crop. It functions as green manure when it is plowed back into the earth before it goes to seed. Mustard plants also attract garden pests. Harmful

Green in Snow		From northern China; mild flavor; good in winter greenhouses, early spring, late fall
India mustard		Semiclosed head, large leaves on broad thick stems; lots of mustard taste
Leaf Heading	Chinese Leaf mustard	Large light green leaves; sweet and tender
Miike Giant	Giant Japanese Tendergreen	Thick dark green leaves, crumpled and frilled; pungent
Miike Purple	Japanese mustard	Purple, clear peppery taste
Old Fashion	Old Fashion Ragged Edge mustard; Hen Peck	Long, ruffed leaves; superb for salads
Slobolt	new in 1987	Smooth, dark green leaves
Southern Giant Curled	Southern Curled	Large, bright green leaves with crumpled frilled edges; mild, mustardy flavor

Source: *Garden Seed Inventory,* 3rd edition, 1992.

The Faith of a Seed

The kingdom of heaven is like to a grain of mustard seed, which a man took, and sowed in his field: Which indeed is the least of all seeds: but when it is grown, it is the greatest among herbs, and become the tree, so that the birds of the air come and lodge in the branches thereof.

The Bible, New Testament, Matthew

insects are drawn to their volatile oils and lay their eggs on the leaves. The mustard plants are then removed, the unhatched eggs along with them, before the pests can harm the crops. Mustard is particularly effective in attracting insects away from cabbage, cauliflower, radish, kohlrabi, Brussels sprouts, turnips, and collard greens. It is often planted between rows of fruit trees and grapevines where it will also draw insects from the crops, but commercial gardeners warn that it should be used with care and removed before it goes to seed. Mustard naturalizes in a single generation and, because its seed is so hardy, it can become an annoying weed. Wild mustard can be effectively broken, and thus controlled, by rolling a field—a technique common in farming—early in the day, while the mustard is still wet from the morning's dew. The secretions of mustard's roots help balance an acid soil, and although the white and black varieties are said to reduce populations of nematodes (parasitic worms found in some soils), they also deplete nonacid soil.

How many, say, potatoes does it take to make a pound? Two, perhaps three, if you consider russets, or a dozen or so if you use small new red potatoes or Yellow Finns. How many tomatoes? Three, four, five, fifteen, depending on their type and size. A pound of cherries makes a good bagful, too many to eat in one sitting, except at the start of the season when no one can get enough. Anyone who shops can imagine a pound of almost anything: a dozen and a half thin stalks of asparagus, enough dry spaghetti to fit comfortably in one hand, four sticks of butter, a substantial chunk of cheese.

Now, try this: Imagine a pound of mustard seed. How many tiny yellow seeds, just three millimeters in diameter, does it take to make a handful, a cup, a full pound? One pound of white mustard seed—the largest of the three types of seed—contains approximately 70,000 seeds, or 4,375 seeds per ounce. Just one of those seeds can produce several hundred new seeds during its growing cycle. One begins to understand why mustard seed has been used throughout history as a symbol of fertility.

The Hindu religion in particular identifies the seed as a symbol of fecundity. Early Christians, too, looked to the seed's symbolic possibilities, but used it to express other aspects of their tradition. There are numerous biblical references to the tiny, resilient seed, most of which refer to its size and endurance. All the faith that one needs, Christians read, is as much as a grain of mustard. No doubt the seed was chosen in part because of its astonishing endurance, its innate ability to survive and transcend unfavorable conditions, waiting patiently in the ground until the rain comes in proper amounts and at the right time. Mustard can wait for decades, for as long as a hundred years or more, before sprouting. A mustard seed is full of remarkable power: all of mustard's potential—not just of the plant itself, but its heat and flavor—is contained within the small seed, a tiny miracle of which we avail ourselves with each squirt or spread or bite of mustard. It is no surprise that it has earned a place not only in our culinary history but in world mythology as well.

It is the outer shell, or husk, of the mustard seed that gives it its strength. A tough coating protects the interior heart and gives the seed the color by which it is known. What is called white mustard, Brassica *alba*, is actually a pale tan or pale yellow, frequently with the slightest blush of rose. Brassica *juncea* is known as brown mustard, and its seed is often a deep, rosy brown, although it can be nearly black. To confuse the matter, there is a yellow variety of this brown mustard, which is called, in the commercial mustard industry, oriental mustard. Black mustard, Brassica *nigra*, is close to the same size as brown mustard, and its color is a rosy brown rather than a true black. The seed itself is oval rather than round. Today, black mustard plays no significant role in the world mustard market. It is not grown commercially in North America and is cultivated in only a few places in the rest of the world. The seedpods of this mustard shatter easily, thus requiring it to be carefully harvested by hand. It is not profitable to grow mustard on a large scale in this manner, particularly when brown and oriental mustards have such similar qualities that even experts can be fooled.

Mustard's hard husk must be broken for mustard to sprout or release its flavor and heat. In the ground, or under a damp cloth in your kitchen, the interior of the seed absorbs water until the heart swells enough to burst open the shell and the tiny sprout begins to grow. A taste of a mustard sprout provides the full impact of mustard's heat.

Inside the mustard seed, the heart is made up of the endosperm and the bran. The mustard flour, or dry mustard, that most of us have seen is the endosperm ground to a fine powder, with the husk and bran sifted out. All mustard flour, once these other elements are removed, is yellow, although brown and oriental mustards are yellower than both yellow and white mustards. It is this mustard flour that is available to the home cook. Whole mustard seeds, crushed and sold as ground mustard, are available to the commercial food industry. Some of the ground mustard is used in salad dressings and sauces, but most goes into sausages and other prepared meat products. In all these products, it is used not only for the flavor it imparts but also for its binding and emulsifying abilities. It is mustard's bran that is primarily responsible for its ability to bind a sauce, although the mustard flour itself absorbs twice its weight in water and one and a half times its weight in oil, so it too helps thicken a mixture such as a vinaigrette or a sauce.

Today, much of the world's mustard seed is grown on the Canadian plains, where the hot, dry summer offers the best environment for the maturing and harvesting of the seed, which is cut by a combine. The northern plains of the United States also produce commercial mustard crops, but not nearly enough to supply even national demand for the seed. The United States is the second major importer of Canadian mustard, purchasing the majority of Canada's white mustard seed crop. France, where little commercial mustard is grown today, buys the largest quantity, purchasing primarily Canadian brown mustard.

Types of Mustard Seed, their History, and their Uses			
SCIENTIFIC NAME	*Brassica hirta*	*Brassica juncea*	*Brassica nigra*
COMMON NAME	White	Brown	Black
OTHER NAMES	*Sinapis alba; Brassica alba;* Yellow	Black, Oriental, Asian, indian	*Sinapis nigra;* **Brown**
PLACE OF ORIGIN	Eastern Mediterranean	Himalayas	Persia (Iran)
CURRENT CULTIVATION	North America, England, Europe	North America, England, Europe, Russia	India, Nepal, Sicily, Ethiopia
COLOR OF HUSK	Pale tan to pale yellow	Yellow; brown to dark brown or black	Dark; purplish brown with red tones
CHARACTERISTICS	Largest seed; round; mildest heat felt only on tongue	Medium seed; **round,. intense** heat felt on tongue and in **eyes, nose, sinuses**	Smallest seed; oval; difficult to **harvest; intense** heat felt on tongue and in **eyes, nose, sinuses**
ACTIVE CHEMICAL AGENTS	Myrosin reacts with sinalbin to produce acrinyl isothiocyanate	Myrosin reacts with sinigrin to produce allyl isothiocyanate	Myrosin reacts with sinigrin to produce allyl isothiocyanate
HISTORICAL USES	English dry; Alsace; Lorraine	Mustard oil; Dijon; Bordeaux, Meaux; other European	English dry; Dijon; Bordeaux, Meaux; other European
CURRENT USES	Ballpark; English dry, mild mustard flour (retail), sprouts; ground mustard used in commercially processed meats	Mustard oil; English dry, Chinese style, Dijon and most other French and European, hot mustard flour (retail), sprouts	Limited because of difficulty of cultivation and harvest
GREENS USED	As cover crops and green manure, gathered wild in spring	Commercial mustard greens	Gathered wild in spring
RETAIL AVAILABILITY	Whole seeds, mustard flour, prepared	Whole seeds, mustard flour, prepared; greens; oil	Virtually unavailable

The National Mustard Museum

Today, the National Mustard Museum is located in downtown Middleton, Wisconsin, where it moved in 2009, when it also changed its name from the Mount Horeb Mustard Museum. It hosts an annual National Mustard Day celebration in August.

In late 2014, there were nearly six thousand mustards in the collection, representing fifty states and seventy countries. The museum is open seven days a week, admission is free, and, yes, it includes a story.

The history of the museum is as unlikely as it is charming. In October of 1986, Barry Levenson was depressed. The Red Sox had just lost the World Series and Barry soothed himself by wandering the aisles of a twenty-four-hour supermarket. I need a hobby, he thought to himself in the 3:00 a.m. darkness, and when he passed the mustard section, Mount Horeb Mustard Museum folklore tells us, he had a vision. "If you collect us, they will come," he heard, whispered perhaps by a spunky little jar of mustard longing for the limelight. He spent the thirteen dollars or so he had in his pocket and thus began what has become the world's largest collection of prepared mustards.

At that time, Barry was an assistant attorney general for the state of Wisconsin, working in the criminal appeals division. He continued his dual existence, prosecutor by day, mustard collector by night, until 1991, when he resigned his full-time career position to work full time on his collection of mustards and mustard memorabilia.

In 1989, Barry opened the Mount Horeb Mustard Museum; in April 1992, the museum was moved to its current location in what has to be one of the grandest openings in history. Standing at the door of the new location, Barry turned to his wife, Pat, with that immortal request, "Please pass the mustard." She turned and repeated the request, and on and on it went through the line of over three hundred mustard fanatics braving a rainstorm to assist in the historic passing of the final jar of the mustard collection from the old museum to the new. When the request reached the old museum, associate curator Judy LeMasters started the plastic twenty-four-ounce squeeze jar of Plochman's yellow mustard toward its new home, while the mustard passers chanted, "Mustard si, mayo no," and several rhymes celebrating the world's most popular condiment.

In addition to being museum curator and editor of its newsletter, The Proper Mustard, Barry Levenson is a mustard maker. He began with a single type, a cinnamon honey mustard made with prepared Dijon, and he gave it as gifts to his friends. Everyone loved it. Barry had a label made and then decided he should have a line of products, three mustards under the brand Slimm & Nunne, since, he says, those are your chances of finding a better mustard. He added Golden Ginger Mustard and Kerala Curry Mustard, and finally decided he should make a mustard from scratch. He began with whole seeds, added beer, malt vinegar, and spices, and gave the world Slimm & Nunne's Grainy Gusto Mustard. Slimm & Nunne also launched what may be the world's only numbered, limited edition mustard, Grainy Gusto made with Garten Brau dark beer from Capital Brewery of Middleton, Wisconsin. In spring 1993, John Wagner & Sons took over production and distribution of Barry's mustard, renaming it Mount Horeb Mustard Museum Mustard.

The rest, as they say, is history. One of these days, I hope to see my favorite mustard, PIC, a brand of Dijon from the South of France, among their vast selections.

There is no question that it was the French who both perfected and popularized the preparation of mustard as a condiment. Although recipes for a paste similar to modern mustard appear as early as A.D. 42, mustard was not widely used as a condiment in either Greece or Rome. The Romans introduced the seed to eastern Gaul in the region now known as Bourgogne, or Burgundy, with its well-known capital of Dijon, and from there it spread throughout western Europe. As early as the ninth century, French monasteries were bringing in considerable income from their mustard preparations. Although accounts of the development of the use of mustard in France are contradictory, records exist that allow us to assemble at least a skeleton of mustard's rise to prominence as the world's most popular condiment. With our imagination, we can add the flesh, the sinew, the beating heart, and the blood. There is no dearth of detail, however anecdotal, to inspire us.

Alexandre Dumas, in *Le Grand Dictionnaire de Cuisines*, paints a vivid portrait of thirteenth-century Parisian sauce hawkers. They ran through the streets of Paris at dinnertime, he tells us, crying, "Mustard sauce! . . . Garlic sauce! . . . Scallion sauce! . . . Verjuice sauce! . . . Ravigote sauce! . . ." Parisians eager for sauces for their meat opened their windows and called their preference to the peddlers. Whether or not there was mustard in Dijon at the time, whether the cries were heard only on the streets of Paris or also along Dijon's rue de la Liberte, we can envision modern mustard in its early years.

In the year 1254, secular vinegar makers were granted permission to make mustard as well as vinegar. By 1292, the Parisian tax register listed ten *moutardiers*. At the same time, the mixture that would eventually become the touchstone for French mustard was being developed in Dijon. There, the first written reference came in 1336 and the first regulations governing its production in 1390. At that time, it was stated simply that the mustard must be soaked in and mixed with good vinegar, as opposed to spoiled wine, as was often the practice. In addition, it was required to age for twelve days before being sold.

The next several decades saw an increase in the regulation of mustard and its makers, the creation of inspectors, and the formation of mustard-maker guilds and corporations. Still, it seems that adulteration and contamination persisted until the middle of the sixteenth century, when regulations were instituted governing the cleanliness of all utensils used in the production of mustard. In 1658, additional laws protected mustard producers, making it an offense for anyone else to make the sauce. A substantial fine and the confiscation of the unauthorized product rendered it unprofitable for others to attempt to compete with the official mustard makers of France.

In spite of the wide acceptance of mustard and the regulations governing its production, it appears that its popularity was on the decline in the early eighteenth century. The House of Maille, founded in 1747, was doing well in Paris, but general interest in the condiment had ebbed, in part because of competition from spices newly available from the Americas and the Far East. The market was revived, and the city of Dijon as the capital of mustard secured, when, in 1856, Burgundian Jean Naigeon substituted *verjuice* for the vinegar that had been used in nearly all French mustard preparations. The use of verjuice–the juice of unripe grapes–resulted in a mustard that was less acidic and less pungent than France had tasted before, and thus the smooth, suave condiment assumed its place in history.

By this time, many of the proprietors whose names we recognize on today's mustard labels were setting up shop and the revived interest in mustard allowed room for them all. The House of Maille, which currently offers eight flavored mustards, then had twenty-four varieties, including nasturtium mustard, anchovy mustard, garlic mustard, and mustard with truffles. The enduring house, which today is part of a conglomerate that includes Grey Poupon, supplied mustard to Madame de Pompadour. The House of Bordin, Maille's main competitor, offered forty different mustards, including varieties flavored with rose, with vanilla, and with garlic. In 1777, the company that would become known as Grey Poupon was founded, although Maurice Grey did not arrive on the scene until 1834 and his partner, Auguste Poupon, not until 1866. Grey revolutionized the mustard industry when he invented new machinery that greatly streamlined the production of mustard without sacrificing its quality. With his new automation, production rose from about thirty-five pounds a day per person to over a hundred pounds per day. The company flourished, and when Napoleon III ate mustard, it bore the name Grey Poupon.

Alexandre Bornibus, a Burgundian who established himself as a Parisian mustard maker, became fashionable not only for the taste and variety of his mustards, but for two distinct types, men's mustard and ladies' mustard. It was his claim that a "lady's palate" was more delicate and sensitive than a man's and thus typical Dijon mustard was too strong for women. Accurate or not, this distinction drew a great deal of attention to the new mustard maker. Bornibus was obviously quite adept at marketing, and Alexander Dumas's lengthy essay on mustard, which he claimed was inspired by an anonymous correspondent who forced a public response by not including a return address, was actually an advertisement commissioned by the astute Paris businessman. The article, originally published in 1873, concludes with the author's chance discovery of Bornibus's mustards and his delight upon tasting them. Bornibus's original little shop at 60 boulevard de la Villette survives today and is run by his direct descendants.

Mustard's popularity continued to flourish in the nineteenth century, but the number of mustard makers began a steady decline as large companies absorbed smaller producers. In 1865, there were thirty-nine mustard manufacturers in Dijon; by 1911, there were ten. All the while, the French government continued to regulate the industry closely, and in 1937, the regulations were strengthened into laws. Only black mustard or brown mustard can be used in French mustards, except in Alsace and Lorraine, where a preparation of white mustard is traditional. Verjuice, wine, and wine vinegar are the permitted liquids, and spices, salt, water, and sulphur dioxide can be added. If the prepared mustard contains any other ingredients—flour, white mustard seed, or flour, eggs, oil—it must be labeled as a condiment and not as a mustard. At this same time, Dijon was granted an *appellation contrôlée,* or designation of origin once granted only to wines. Although the designation requires a specific method rather than a location of production, nearly all Dijon mustard comes from Dijon and its surrounding area.

Louis XIV granted mustard a coat of arms,
a golden funnel on an azure background.

Other regions of France developed their own styles of mustard, but none succeeded in capturing the favor of the rest of the country, or indeed, of the world, like the mustard of Dijon. Just two other styles remain popular today. Pommery is perhaps the brand most familiar to us. This is the whole grain mustard of Meaux, characterized by its sharp vinegar flavor and crunchy whole mustard seeds. The Pommery family took over the company in 1760, and their mustard is said to have been praised by noted connoisseur Jean Anthelme Brillat-Savarin as the finest in the world. The mustard of Bordeaux, similarly coarse-grained and tart although spicier than that of Meaux, remains a popular condiment today, as well.

Pope John XXII appointed a lazy and arrogant nephew to the position of "chief mustard maker," thus coining a phrase that endures today to indicate a vain and stupid person.

He a good wit! hang him baboon! His wit is as thick as Tewkesbury mustard.

—Falstaff, in William Shakespeare's Henry IV

The Romans probably introduced mustard to the English as well as to the French, although the history of the spice is harder to trace once it reaches England. Shakespeare mentions a mustard made in Tewkesbury in the sixteenth century, but no records of the once flourishing business survive today. The seeds of Tewskesbury mustard were washed, pounded, and sifted, and the resulting mustard flour was mixed with cold water infused with horseradish. The mustard was shaped into balls that were then dried, making them easy to transport and to store. To prepare the mustard, a piece was broken off and reconstituted with a liquid: buttermilk, vinegar, beer, red wine, cherry juice, or cider. Occasionally other flavorings–spices, honey, sugar–were added. The resulting mustard was very thick and very hot. As popular as Tewkesbury mustard was for a time, it disappeared suddenly, with no written record and no specific recipes left behind.

It wasn't long before another English region spawned a celebrity mustard maker. Mrs. Clements of Durham became enormously popular

The History of a Condiment

Clean the mustard seed very carefully. Sift it well and wash in cold water. After it is clean, soak it in cold water two hours. Stir it, squeeze it, and put into a new, or very clean, mortar. Crush it with a pestle. When it is well ground, put the resulting paste in the centre of the mortar, press and flatten it with the hand. Make furrows in the surface and put hot coals in them. Pour water with saltpetre over these. This will take the bitterness out of the seed and prevent it from moulding. Pour off the moisture completely. Pour strong white vinegar over the mustard, mix it thoroughly with the pestle, and force through a sieve.

Columella, *De Re Rustica*, A.D. 42

when she took to grinding mustard seeds and sifting them through fine cloth exactly as if she were milling wheat. Although she was not the first to process mustard in this way, she seems to have been the most industrious. She kept her method and her recipe secret, and built up a very successful mustard trade until she sold her business to King George I.

Although other mustard companies flourished in England, most notably Keen & Sons, founded in 1747, the next English mustard producer to make an enduring name for himself would not come along until 1804. In that year, Jeremiah Colman, a miller of flour, began the first of several expansions that would make his name a synonym for mustard. Today, we recognize the bright yellow tins of ground mustard that sit on nearly every market shelf in the country. Colman's is a name synonymous with English mustard, just as Dijon is synonymous with French mustard.

Colman's technique was similar to that of Mrs. Clements and the crucial element was that the mustard seed was ground without heating it, so that there was no subsequent release of oil that heating would cause. Today, Colman's mustard is prepared by much the same process that Jeremiah Colman developed. Two types of mustard seed, white and brown, are ground separately and sifted through silk cloth to separate the husks and the bran from the mustard flour. Originally, black mustard seed was used, but it was replaced by brown several decades ago. After grinding and sifting, the two types of mustard are mixed together and packaged in the famous yellow tins. This blend of the two types of mustard provides a full range of sensation on the tongue, along with the pungent, vaporizing effects created only by the brown mustard.

Colman's greatest contribution, and the reason for his company's rapid expansion, was not necessarily mustard itself, although it did and does turn out a consistent high quality product. More importantly, Colman was brilliant at promoting his mustard. The company's packaging is striking: the name Colman's appears in red letters on a bright yellow background, with the signature bull's head alongside.

The image is bold and memorable. In addition to striking graphics, effective advertising campaigns captured the public's attention. The most dramatic campaign was the creation of the Mustard Club (see sidebar). The company produced special mustard tins each Christmas for over fifty years, along with illustrated children's books that were given away during the holiday season. Although Colman's made its name with its mustard flour, still its most popular product, it introduced other preparations beginning in 1933. In that year, Colman's created the first food product sold in a tube, a prepared mustard. Today, the company makes several types of prepared mustards, including a Dijon-style preparation, but none compete in either quality or popularity with Colman's dry mustard.

One of the more surprising aspects of contemporary commercial mustard production is the amount of secrecy that surrounds the industry. Perhaps because the variables in mustard production are so limited, mustard makers guard their individual secrets like precious gems kept hidden far from the light of day. A visit to a large mustard-processing plant in all likelihood reveals no privileged information at all, yet it is virtually impossible to gain access. All mustard is made in relatively the same way. The seed must be crushed, its hull and bran sifted out or not, depending on the type of mustard being made. It then may or may not go through further grinding and crushing. A liquid such as water, wine, vinegar, beer, or a combination of several of these liquids must be added, along with seasonings and perhaps other flavorings. The mustard must be mixed and in some cases simmered and then cooled. Some mustard is aged in large containers before it is bottled, but eventually all of it is put into some sort of container to be shipped to its customer.

None of the subtle details—the specific spices or their amounts, the type of liquid, the quantity of salt or the lack thereof—can be detected by observing the process, yet one is almost always refused access. The recipe for Grey Poupon, now owned domestically by R. J. R. Nabisco, Inc., is kept in a locked safe at all times, and it is said that no one ever speaks about it. That Grey Poupon is now made in California in addition to France—a fact that many would consider an asset—is closely guarded, played down, not advertised. Smaller producers, those who make mustards for a variety of labels, for example, are more generous about whom they allow to observe the mixing and the blending, the boiling and the bottling.

The Mustard Club

There is something about mustard that inspires zaniness, a sort of goofy pursuit of a mustard obsession, a phenomenon I have encountered previously only with garlic. This silliness is not a recent development. The Mustard Club and its adjunct, the Order of the Bath, stand out as the most dramatic and sophisticated examples of the humor that so often surrounds the condiment.

In May 1922, noted British author Dorothy L. Sayers accepted a position as copywriter with one of London's largest advertising agencies, Benson's. Among the projects she worked on was a large campaign commissioned by Colman's. The Mustard Club was the focus of the agency's efforts. The club was full of Sayers's signature talent not only for pun, parody, and rampant good humor; but also for intelligence and historical resonance. The far-reaching campaign included a mock lawsuit against a restaurant for not making its mustard fresh daily and a prospectus of the Mustard Club credited Aesculapius, the god of medicine, with being its original founder. The club's officers in particular bear the mark of the creator of everybody's favorite detective, the charming Lord Peter Wimsey. Among the fictional participants were Master Mustard; Lord Bacon of Cookham; the Baron de Beef, president of the club; and Miss Di Gester; its secretary. A short film produced at the time immortalizes the characters during the trial of a man accused of attempting to eat a ham sandwich without mustard. The crucial evidence is given by the sandwich itself; the offender is found guilty and condemned to soak in a mustard bath, to which he is promptly escorted.

The club published the *Recipe Book of the Mustard Club*, also penned by Dorothy Sayers, who was herself an accomplished cook. Although the club began as a marketing gimmick and without membership solicitation, hundreds of mustard enthusiasts wrote to request membership and were accommodated. A card game was developed, as were several club songs and a monthly newsletter. The Mustard Club became quite fashionable and was the feature of many news items and cartoons of its time. The campaign was considered one of Benson's great successes, and it certainly did the trick, focusing attention and glamour on a humble condiment. The club lasted for seven years, and vanished during the difficult years of the Depression.

The spirit of the Mustard Club has been revived today by Barry Levenson and a score of other mustard producers whose recipe brochures often reveal as much about their humor as they do about mustard itself.

Mustard in the Kitchen

Mustard in the kitchen has three primary functions: as a condiment, as a flavoring agent or spice, and as a vegetable when one includes pickled mustard root, mustard greens, mustard sprouts, and certain other members of the large Cruciferae family. Although both dry and prepared mustards serve as condiments and flavoring agents, they have vastly different characteristics. It is important to understand and use them correctly. Mustard also has good emulsifying ability. It can help bind a sauce, and is used commercially to create the proper texture in sausages and prepared meat products.

As condiments, prepared commercial or homemade mustards are used just as they are, out of the jar or bottle to enhance sandwiches and other prepared foods. A simple piece of grilled fish is enlivened by a spoonful of your favourite mustard, and certain foods—roast beef in England, for example, and sausages in Germany—are rarely served without a spoonful or more of mustard on the side. It takes no particular skill or knowledge to use mustard in this way, simply access to a good selection of condiments and a lively palate that appreciates mustard's good flavor.

The use of mustard flour as a condiment is most common in Asian cuisine, where the flour made from brown seeds is mixed with water or rice vinegar to form the hot spicy sauce we all recognize when we order, say, egg rolls. Mustard in this form is hot and sharp, without the nuance and subtlety of more suave European preparations. It serves its purpose in the same way that wasabi, the Japanese horseradish served with sushi and sashimi, offers a bright flash, a counterpoint to the richness of raw fish, or the way mustard complements the rich textures and flavors of an egg roll, both palate cleansers with a strong punch. Again, it takes no special skill and little knowledge to prepare mustard in this way. The one thing to remember is that the liquid—water or vinegar—should be as cold as possible. Mustard flour mixed with a warm or hot liquid will be bitter.

Mustard as a flavoring agent requires a little more knowledge to use skillfully. To use prepared mustard in this way, be sure to begin with a product whose flavor you like. Although there are scores, hundreds actually, of prepared mustards and mustard condiments available in the retail marketplace, just a few should be considered for use in this way. Certainly, choose whatever you like as a condiment, but it is not necessary to use flavored and generally expensive specialty mustards in most cooking. I keep three or four Dijon mustards and two or three coarse-grain mustards in my pantry for general cooking purposes (see The Annotated Mustard Pantry, page 34), usually adding other ingredients such as honey, green peppercorns, jalapeños, lemon juice, herbs, and spices separately. Not only is this a less expensive way to cook, but it also, I believe, produces the best results because you control both the amount of each ingredient and its freshness. If you want your final dish to taste of tarragon, for example, add fresh tarragon rather than a tarragon mustard. The flavors will be brighter, fresher, and cleaner.

To maintain maximum flavor, mustard should be added later rather than earlier in the cooking process, as heat destroys much of mustard's distinctive taste. Mustard also should be added with a keen awareness of the balance of flavors. A delicate beurre blanc is delightful with a small amount of Dijon-style mustard added—a teaspoon, perhaps—but more would overwhelm the sauce. On the other hand, a teaspoon of prepared mustard would barely be noticed in a heartier mixture like a marinade and substantially more would need to be added.

Mustard flour is part of many a spice cabinet, where it is used in Indian spice mixtures, pickling spice (both the seed and mustard flour), and as part of countless traditional recipes such as gingerbread and chocolate cake. It contributes a richness and a depth of flavor that is not necessarily identified as mustard, but is essential nonetheless. There are many claims that mustard flour heightens the flavors of all foods, much as monosodium glutamate does. Although the statement never has been scientifically verified, it is often the case that mustard appears in unlikely recipes and perhaps this is why. Generally, mustard flour is used as you use other spices and requires no special treatment.

In salad dressings and other emulsified sauces, mustard contributes not only its flavor and its heat, but also its ability to hold an oil and water mixture in suspension. It can help keep a hollandaise sauce or a homemade mayonnaise from separating, and a vinaigrette with a substantial amount of mustard—either dry or prepared—will stay blended longer than a sauce without it.

Mustard & Health

Like most foods with ancient roots, mustard has been heralded as a curative with a variety of healing properties. It also has been reviled, however briefly, as a poison and its advocates dismissed as lunatics. The source of these latter claims are harder to substantiate than the claims of mustard's healing effects, many of which can be readily documented today.

Mustard stimulates appetite and digestion, and it clears the sinuses in much the same way as chilies, which are said to be as effective as nearly all commercial decongestants.

It is a preservative and inhibits the growth of a variety of yeasts, molds, and bacteria. It increases blood circulation, hence its use as mustard plaster, a dressing used to bring increased blood flow to inflamed areas of the body. In the past, it has been used to treat asthma, bronchitis, pleurisy, and pneumonia. Although mustard has generally been taken orally or applied directly to the skin in the form of a mustard plaster, mustard baths are said to be curative, too. Mustard's stimulating effects work in this medium, although the one commercially available mustard bath, Dr. Singha's, is so full of the scents of wintergreen and eucalyptus that it smells like a sickroom. Even so, it is an unbeatable remedy for chilled feet on a winter day. Mustard flour sprinkled in your socks is said to save your toes from frostbite, a claim that is also made about cayenne pepper and other spices containing volatile oils. Indeed, there are mixtures of mustard, ginger, and cayenne pepper that are sold to winter hikers and skiers as foot-warming preparations. They work, up to a point.

Native Americans in the western United States had particularly inter-esting uses for the herb they found growing wild in the Rocky Mountain regions. They used mustard to fight cold symptoms and headaches, to counter sciatic pain, to bring on menstruation, to ease the difficulty of childbirth, and to subdue the causes and discomfort of swollen testicles. Native Americans were aware also of mustard's effectiveness as an emetic, and learned to rinse wild mustard cabbage in several water baths before eating it.

Mustard was once an ingredient in smelling salts, and in ancient times mustard seeds were chewed to relieve the symptoms of toothache. Today, those remedies that take advantage of mustard's stimulating qualities—of the blood and of the appetite—remain relevant, although they are used less than they once were.

Mustard oil concentrates many of mustard's health benefits and may reduce the risk of cancer and cardiovascular disease. It reduces inflammation and discourages both bacteria and fungi. When rubbed on the chest, it can ease the symptoms of cold and flu. It has long been used in massage and, because it has high levels of Vitamin E, is beneficial to both our hair and skin.

A secondary benefit of mustard is that it provides a tremendous amount of flavor for very few calories, just 4.3 per gram. It has no cholesterol or trace amounts of vegetable fat and is between 25 and 32 percent protein. Leaf mustard is particularly rich in vitamins A and C and in calcium (about as much as milk), and also contains considerable amounts of Vitamin B, phosphorus, and magnesium.

Menu for Mustard Tasting

For each taster:
> A small bowl full of thin pretzel sticks
> A large glass of unflavored sparkling water
> An evaluation sheet (see Tasting Notes, page 281) and a pencil
> A napkin

For the table:
> Up to one dozen different mustards
> Ramekins or custard cups filled with three or four tablespoons of the mustards to be tasted, placed in front of their corresponding jars of mustard
> > Bottles or pitchers of chilled sparkling water
> > Additional pretzel sticks

Mustard Tasting

Organized tastings of foods and food products have grown in popularity for the last number of years. A gourmet shop offers samples of several different raspberry vinegars; friends gather together to taste a half-dozen boutique olive oils; farmers' markets hold special tastings of summer's fruits and vegetables. It is a very good marketing tool, a way to introduce customers to new items and to educate them as to what they like and don't like and why. A good tasting is one where you learn something, not just chow down on free goodies.

Such a tasting is also an excellent way for friends to navigate the multitude of new food products appearing on shelves throughout the country. Faced with scores of new olive oils, many of them quite expensive, dozens of unfamiliar vinegars, hundreds of mustards, how is the consumer to make intelligent choices without depleting the food budget? I always suggest that a group of food lovers get together, coordinate their choices so that no brand is duplicated, and organize a tasting. It keeps expenses to a minimum while offering the opportunity to taste a whole pantryful of new products. With mustards, it is an inexpensive, interesting, and delicious occasion, even somewhat refreshing and invigorating. Whereas olive oil and vinegar tastings often leave the palate exhausted and the tasters informed but exhausted or overwhelmed, a mustard tasting can conclude with a hearty feast if everyone is so inclined. Mustard is an appetite stimulant, and we can consume a fair amount of the pungent sauce before we tire.

To taste mustards, gather together all of the ingredients listed in the tasting menu. The pretzel sticks serve as "spoons" for sampling the mustard. Take a little of one mustard on a pretzel stick and then taste the mustard from the pretzel. Don't eat the pretzel at the same time because its texture and flavor will interfere with your experience of the mustard. Discard the pretzel after each taste of mustard. It is helpful to refresh your palate with sparkling water after every couple of tastes. Continue the tasting until everyone has become familiar with all of the mustards and made appropriate notes.

What do we look for when tasting mustard? Although taste is largely subjective, there are certain objective criteria to consider when evaluating the condiment. First of all, the mustard should be entirely pleasant. It should be somewhat acidic, but not overly so, and it should not be too salty. Its flavors should be well balanced, with no single element dominating. If it is sweet, for example, sugar should not be the predominant taste, merely an element of the whole. The texture should be smooth or, in the case of coarse-grain mustard, pleasantly grainy, not gritty or hard. It should have a fairly thick consistency, so that it easily holds its own shape on a spoon, but it should not be so thick as to be cloying or tongue-coating. Mustard should not taste floury, musty, or metallic; nor should it taste or smell eggy. Even if it is hot, it should not burn the tongue. Mustard always should have a pleasant aftertaste, a harmonious finish on the palate as the flavors fade together. If it vaporizes so that your eyes water and forehead sweats but you are eager for more, consider yourself lucky and be sure to write down the name of that mustard.

When tasting for comparison, taste mustards of a similar type, all Dijon, for example, or all sweet-hot. Judge Dijon mustards for their smooth texture, the balance of acid, the depth of flavor. If tasting to discover new mustards, simply choose ones you have been wanting to try or those that seem interesting. Mustards, unlike, say, vinegars or wines, will not compete with or overwhelm each other.

COMMERCIAL MUSTARDS			
Type	Characteristics	Recommended Storage	Uses
Flour, mild (one of the standard retail dry mustards)	Pale yellow powder, heat on tongue	Pantry, well sealed against dampness	Mild homemade mustard; as a spice; pickling
Flour, hot (one of the standard retail dry mustards)	Deep yellow powder, full vaporizing heat	Pantry, well sealed against dampness	Chinese-style mustard; homemade mustards; as a spice in sauces, dressings; pickling
Colman's Dry	Mix of mild and hot mustard flours	Pantry, well sealed against dampness	English hot mustard; Chinese-style mustard; homemade mustards; as a spice in sauces, dressings; pickling
Seeds, white	Pale yellow seeds	Pantry, well sealed against dampness	Homemade coarse-grain mustard; pickling; Indian spice blends; garnish; sprouts
Seeds, brown	Tiny reddish black seeds	Pantry, well sealed against dampness	Homemade Dijon-style mustard; Indian spice blends; sprouts
American yellow	Sharply acidic but without much heat; made from white mustard seeds only	Refrigeration is not essential, but will help maintain maximum flavor	The basic hotdog mustard
American brown	Mild with a bit of spiciness, less acidic than American yellow	Refrigeration is not essential, but will help maintain maximum flavor	As a condiment if you prefer a very mild mustard
English hot	Full taste on the tongue and full vaporization; very hot	Refrigeration is not essential, but will help maintain n1aximurn flavor	As a condiment with smoked meats, Cheddar cheese, sausages, roast beef
Dijon	Typical Dijon that has been toned down some	Refrigeration is not essential, but will help maintain maximum flavor	As a condiment, in marinades, sauces, dressings

Dijon, extra strong, for export	Smooth, suave French mustard, more pungent than Dijon, but less so than that produced for domestic use (in France)	Refrigeration is not essential, but will help maintain maximum flavor	As a condiment; in marinades, sauces, dressings
Dijon, extra-forte, French	Smooth, suave French mustard with full range of pungency	Refrigeration is not essential, but will help maintain maximum flavor	As a condiment; in marinades, sauces, dressings
Bordeaux	Made with whole brown seeds, sweet, spicy, tart	Pantry	As a condiment, on sandwiches, with smoked meats and pates
Meaux	Made with whole brown seeds, slightly spicy, very tart, not sweet	Pantry	As a condiment, on sandwiches, with smoked meats and pâtés
German hot	Brown, often hot, frequently sweet, and often flavored with horseradish	Refrigeration is not essential, but will help maintain maximum flavor	As a condiment with sausages, smoked meats, pates
Creole	Vary with producer, most often slightly coarse-grain brown mustard, rather tart	Refrigeration may not be essential, but will help maintain flavor; check ingredients list	As a condiment
Dijon style	Many have an unpleasant floury texture, generally inferior in all ways to French mustards	Refrigeration is not essential, but will help maintain maximum flavor	Limited, unless you find one you particularly like
Flavored Dijon style	Quality and characteristics vary greatly, as do flavors; those made with true Dijon tend to be best	Refrigeration often essential; check ingredients list	As a condiment
Other flavored mustards	Quality and characteristics vary greatly	Refrigeration often essential; check ingredients list	As a condiment

PART II
The Annotated Mustard Pantry

I t is easy for either the enthusiastic or the reluctant home cook to keep a helpful supply of good mustards in the pantry, and there are several important reasons to do so. First, if you want to incorporate a variety of mustards into your cooking, you should have them at hand, rather than having to run to the market when a recipe calls for them. The mustards I recommend here should allow you to complete nearly any recipe requiring mustard. Second, a comprehensive supply of mustards will help you grow as a cook. With them at your fingertips, there on your shelf each time you open the pantry, they will inspire you. You will become adept at using them, and that use will start to bear your signature. Finally, mustards are great in an emergency. If friends show up unexpectedly, if you can't get to the market for a few days, a good supply of mustards will assist you in almost any culinary emergencies that arise.

Mustard Labels

In general, it is a good idea to get into the habit of reading the labels of the foods we buy, particularly the ingredients portion. Names of products can be deceptive, especially with something like mustard, which has no legal definition, unlike, say, vinegar. If a product is labeled simply "vinegar," United States law requires that it be apple cider vinegar and nothing else. A product labeled as mustard has no such legal guarantee. It may include vinegar, wine, beer, oil, eggs, flour, and any number of spices, additives, or preservatives. Indeed, a product labeled as mustard is not required to contain mustard. I came across such a condiment and when I queried its maker, the response was that the mustard was included in the ingredient listing of "spices." Fortunately, however, there is, in most instances, a larger portion of mustard in products sold as mustard, mustard sauce, or mustard condiment.

Prepared mustard is a simple mixture and should contain only whole mustard seeds, mustard flour, liquid, spices, salt, pepper, and sometimes sugar. It would be helpful if labeling guidelines required that preparations with ingredients other than these be labeled as condiments, but since there is no such requirement, we must be watchful. Additional ingredients influence not only the taste of the product, but the amount of calories, the percentage of those calories that are fat, and the way in which the condiment must be stored.

Flavored mustards in particular may contain any number of ingredients other than those required to make a simple mustard paste. These additional ingredients—eggs, fruits, vegetables, and juices, for example—are often perishable, and condiments containing them should be stored in the refrigerator rather than on the pantry shelf. Although true mustards can be stored in the pantry, it is dangerous to leave all mustard condiments on the shelf without verifying their stability. Over time, mustard loses its pungency; refrigeration will slow the loss of flavor.

It is fashionable these days for a variety of businesses, particularly wineries and specialty stores, to feature their own mustards, although few of these mustards are actually made by the facilities that sell them. Rather, they are produced by large wholesalers who offer specialty labeling. Buy these products when you like them, but remember that they are often more expensive than similar products found in general markets, and don't be fooled into thinking you're choosing a handcrafted product. Only rarely are these condiments made from recipes unique to the businesses whose labels they display.

The Well-Stocked Pantry

A passionate cook should have these mustards on hand. A reluctant cook can get by with just a couple, one for hot dogs and such—French's or Gulden's—and one Dijon.

Dijon:

Three jars of a good Dijon for cooking purposes, with two jars on the pantry shelf for daily usage and one jar in the refrigerator for culinary emergencies (like having forgotten to restock your pantry), one jar of Dijon extra-forte, one or more of the best (i.e., your favorite) Dijons for use as a condiment.

Coarse-grain mustard:

Three types, with one smooth and balanced, one tart, and one sweet.

Flavored:

Those flavored mustards you like in amounts that will be used within four to six months. I keep several mustards flavored with sweet onions, one commercial honey mustard, one green peppercorn mustard, and one Dijon with lemon.

Mustard flour:

Mild, hot, and Colman's.

Seeds:

Yellow and brown.

Other Mustard Products:

Mustard oil and pickled mustard root (optional, except for cooks who love Asian cuisines).

Shopping For Mustards

Certain mustard products are difficult to come by in neighborhood markets. Although you will find mustard flour, and possibly mustard seeds, in the spice section, they will be in small containers, and therefore impractical for use in recipes that may call for as much as a cup or more. A wholesale food distributor that sells directly to the public is your best bet for purchasing mustard seeds and mustard flour in bulk. Natural foods stores often carry these items in bulk as well.

A Glossary of Commercial Mustards

American Brown Mustard The classic delicatessen mustard, this mixture is brown, less tart than ballpark mustard, and mildly spicy but not hot. It is traditionally used in redeye gravy. Gulden's, the oldest mustard brand in America, is the most familiar brand.

American Mustard This mustard accounts for 75 percent of all mustard eaten in the United States. It is made from ground white mustard seeds, turmeric, and vinegar, and has a bright, sharp taste. It certainly belongs on hot dogs, but has limited culinary uses. Plochman's, founded in 1852, and French's, founded in 1904, lead in sales.

Ballpark Mustard Same as American Mustard.

Black Mustard Generally indicates an English prepared mustard made with whole brown seeds, molasses, and sometimes beer.

Chinese Mustard A simple mixture of hot mustard flour and water, with little nuance but lots of fire.

Coarse-Grain Mustard Mustard made, at least in part, with whole mustard seeds; England, Germany, and France all produce distinctive versions. French types tend to be sharply acidic, while English and German are often sweet.

Creole Mustard Although many products may bear this designation, it is generally a simple preparation of coarse-ground seeds, vinegar, and, sometimes, horseradish and sugar.

Dijon A smooth, elegant mustard with an extremely fine texture, a strong but not overbearing acidic element, and a subtle play of herbs and spices; some Dijon mustards can be quite pungent, although those made for export are milder than those made for French consumption.

Dijon, Extra-Forte The same mustard as Dijon, but with its full force of vaporizing pungency.

Dijon-Style Dijon is a protected name, and must be made according to specific guidelines set in 1937 by the French government. Grey Poupon is the only true Dijon mustard made outside of France. Other mustards that attempt to duplicate Dijon's characteristics must be labeled "Dijon style"; some work, most don't.

Mustard Flour, Hot The powdered endosperm of brown mustard, it has mustard's full potency. Mustard flour is commonly found in the spice sections of retail markets and labeled as mustard, dry mustard, ground mustard, or mustard powder.

Mustard Flour, Mild The powdered endosperm of white mustard. Its heat is felt only on the tongue, and it is often quite bitter if mixed directly with an acid or if it is not allowed sufficient aging. Labeled as mustard, dry mustard, or ground mustard, it is usually found in the spice sections of retail markets.

English Mustard Generally made with a blend of hot and mild mustard flours and with whole seeds, this mustard can be either dry or prepared. Colman's (dry), a blend of white and brown mustard flours, is the best known of the classic English mustards.

Flavored Mustard A mustard condiment that, rather than being made in a particular style (Dijon or Creole, for example), is flavored with any number of herbs, spices, aromatics, vegetables, fruits, or juices.

German Mustard May be coarse-grain or smooth, but most German mustards are hot and often sweet, and brown rather than yellow.

Japanese Mustard Generally refers to a purplish green leafy vegetable that is either a component of salad mixes (when harvested small) or sold separately (when harvested more mature).

Mostarda An Italian condiment, typically made of preserved or dried fruit suspended in a sweet syrup flavored with mustard, especially white mustard seed. It is traditionally served with main courses such as bollito misto but makes a fine accompaniment to roast pork, roasted chicken, and cheddar and similar cheeses.

Mostarda di Cremona The best known of the Italian condiments that combine fruit and a mustard-flavored syrup.

Mustard Oil Generally indicates pure mustard oil extracted from the seed of Brassica *juncea*. Recently a product named mustard oil appeared on the market that is a blend of mustard oil and canola oil flavored with mustard flour. It is quite good.

Mustard Seed, Brown Available commercially in the spice section of many supermarkets, this is the seed of Brassica *juncea*.

Mustard Seed, White This is generally what you get when you buy a product labeled simply as mustard seed. It is the seed of Brassica *alba*, and the one most commonly used in pickling spice.

Mustard-Flavored Oil Any oil that has been flavored with mustard seeds or mustard flour.

Oriental Mustard In the commercial mustard industry, oriental mustard refers to yellow Brassica *juncea* (brown mustard). In common usage, the term refers to a simple paste of water and hot mustard flour.

Pickled Mustard Root The roots of Brassica *juncea* pickled and used in pork balls and other Chinese dishes.

Russian Mustard Generally refers to a sweet mustard made with brown or oriental mustard so that it has its full range of flavor.

Sweet-Hot Mustard There are numerous mustards labelled as sweet-hot and they vary a great deal. Sometimes these mustards are called California-style, named, perhaps, for the number of boutique mustard producers in the state.

PART III
A Mustard Cookbook

Cooking with Mustard

There are thousands of recipes that call for mustard, from simple mixtures of commercial mayonnaise and ballpark mustard combined quickly as a sauce for grilled fish (I had this once, with salmon that had been swimming just a few hours before; it was extraordinary) to complex soups, sauces, stews, breads, and pickles that use one or more of mustard's many culinary properties to enliven them. *What do I want the recipes to offer the reader?* I asked myself over and over, as I added new recipes and discarded old ones, as I revived some and sent others to the alternate file for a second and third time. I wanted, when I first conceived of this book, to present mustard recipes in a historical context, showing how the use of the ubiquitous plant in all its forms—herb, spice, condiment, vegetable—has changed over the centuries, how it has remained the same, the ways in which it continues to inspire cooks from diverse cultures with its pungency and power. There is a historical record that needs to be preserved, I told myself, and classical traditions and recipes that need to be honored.

In certain ways, this book, when first published in 1993, was ahead of the curve when it comes to the American palate. When I struggled one terribly stormy weekend preparing time-honored recipes such as tongue in mustard-vinegar sauce, rabbit stew in a mustard marinade, and chicken livers with coarse-grain mustard, the book began to take the form I wanted. I had lamb's kidneys, plump and perfectly rare, and sweetbreads in a fragrant mustard reduction sauce, and no one at all eager to try either one of them. They were all wonderfully rich and delicious, full of good flavors that evoked an earlier time and style of eating and of thinking. In the 1990s, innards were on few menus and in fewer markets. How happy I am that this has changed, thanks to the new butchery movement and a growing environmental consciousness that honors the entire animal, not just those parts that don't look too much like what they actually are. There is also growing acknowledgement that innards, especially from pastured and grass-fed animals, are quite good for humans.

And so, in a way, everything old *is* new again, including when it comes to classic mustard dishes. Still, *The Good Cook's Book of Mustard* is, as it was when it was first published, a contemporary cookbook, a collection of good recipes that we will use today. It is not an historical record, though history does provide both inspiration and garnishes. But the recipes themselves stand on their own and feature easy-to-find ingredients, a contemporary style and an ease of preparation, always with an eye toward considerations of health, as I interpret them.

Finally, I want to add a word about my philosophy of cooking and of the function of recipes. The requirements of writing and contemporary editing often make a recipe seem cast in stone, as if each specific measurement and technique were of more importance than is often the case. In many instances, there is something arbitrary about the choices a chef makes when committing to paper a particular combination of ingredients or way of blending them. I believe there is more than one way to produce a desired result, and we see this over and over as each cook leaves his or her own signature on every dish. Thus, when I list, say, chutney in a recipe and give no further instructions, do not wonder which chutney I want you to use. Rather, choose a chutney you prefer or discover a new one. Work from the spirit of a recipe, but develop the skill and, most of all, the confidence, to adapt it to your own style and preference.

A Note about Salt

The recipes in this book were tested using a flake salt, specifically Diamond Crystal Kosher Salt, which is reasonably priced and free of additives. It is flakier and less dense than table salt; a recipe that calls for one teaspoon of kosher salt may require only half or three quarters that amount of fine-grain salt, though, honestly, I rarely measure. I salt to taste, using my fingers to add pinch after pinch until it tastes just right. Regarding salt in general, I do not recommend omitting it. Although salt is constantly attacked as unhealthful, only an extremely small segment of the population is adversely affected by its consumption. Salt is an essential seasoning that heightens the taste of nearly all foods; savory foods do not reach their full flavor without its skillful application. Salt draws the disparate elements of a dish together and, because it melts slowly on the tongue, contributes to the harmonious blending of flavors and creates a pleasant finish on the palate.

A Note about Equipment & Tools

Stocking your kitchen, no matter its size, with well-chosen tools is essential if you love to cook. I have written about this in detail in several of my recent books. Your kitchen must be well lit, you should have at least two large wooden cutting boards and two high-quality knives that you sharpen or have sharpened annually. An electronic kitchen scale makes life easier, too, once you get used to weighing ingredients instead of measuring their bulk. A sturdy pepper mill and a salt pig or salt box that allows you to grab pinches are essential, too.

For grinding, I prefer a large suribachi, a Japanese mortar and pestle. If you love to work with whole spices and seeds, including mustard seeds, you may want to invest in an electric spice grinder.

When mixing mustards, always use a nonreactive bowl; glass, porcelain and stainless steel are fine; plastic and aluminum are not. Several sizes of sturdy whisks—a small whisk, a balloon whisk and a long-handled whisk are sufficient—and wooden spoons with thick handles will make your work more pleasant and efficient.

To store mustards and other condiments, you'll need glass jars, not plastic containers.

When it comes to food safety, common sense and a bit of knowledge is your best guide. Don't leave proteins at room temperature for too long, wash your hands and tools, including cutting boards, frequently and clean up as you go. Always choose local ingredients whenever possible and, if you don't have one, find a good butcher, one who can tell you the source of what he or she sells. Factory farming is responsible for nearly all national outbreaks of food-borne illnesses and your best hedge against the problem is to know your farmers and ranchers and to understand their practices.

Starters, Snacks & Nibbles

The simplest mustardy appetizers, yummy little nibbles to whet the appetite, may be little pretzel sticks or jumbo pretzels, hot from the oven, with a jar of your favorite mustard alongside. It's a great way to start a meal, especially a picnic or summer barbecue.

It doesn't take much for a more elaborate presentation: Seasonal vegetables, trimmed into bite-size pieces, with mustard, mustard cream, or any mustard sauce alongside for dipping make a perfect appetizer to share. A homemade or commercial paté—chunky duck paté is one of my favorites and I also love potted chicken livers and a good pork terrine—with thinly shaved onions, cornichons, warm bread, and your best Dijon nearby.

In this chapter, I offer some of my favorite nibblers, those I return to time after time.

Popcorn with Mustard Butter & Cheese
Artichokes with Mustard Mayonnaise
Roasted Asparagus with Prosciutto and Mustard
New Potatoes with Mustard Butter and Mustard Cream
Beet Caviar with Egg Mimosa, Créme Fraiche & Croutons
Rock Shrimp with Remoulade Sauce
Root Vegetable Remoulade with Smoked Salmon

Popcorn
with Mustard Butter & Cheese

Makes about 3 quarts

Really? A recipe for popcorn? Yes. Thanks to the microwave, so many people have forgotten both why and how to make popcorn on top of the stove. The why is easy: Popcorn cooked on top of the stove tastes better and is a much healthier choice than microwaved popcorn, which frequently contains toxic chemicals and other additives.

The how isn't difficult, either.

But first, what is popcorn, really? It's pretty simple. In certain varieties of corn, water becomes trapped within the molecules of starch and protein. When the kernels are heated, the water vaporizes, expands, and the kernel turns itself inside out, with a pop. Voila! Popcorn!

½ cup Mustard Butter, page 220
3 tablespoons olive oil or corn oil
⅔ cup unpopped corn
Kosher salt
Black pepper in a mill
3 ounces (¾ cup) freshly grated premium cheddar, dry jack, or other grating
    cheese

Put the mustard butter into a small saucepan and set it over low heat; do not let it brown.

Heat the oil in a wide saucepan over medium heat, add the popcorn, agitate the pan, and when the first kernel pops, cover the pot, leaving the lid slightly off center to allow steam, but not popcorn, to escape. Agitate the pan frequently and remove from the heat when the sound of popping has stopped for a full 20 to 30 seconds.

Turn the popcorn into a wide deep bowl, drizzle the butter over it, and toss gently but thoroughly. Season with salt and pepper, toss again, add the cheese, and toss a final time.

Serve right away.

Artichokes
with Mustard Mayonnaise

Serves 4

A born-and-bred California girl, I grew up eating artichokes and they remain one of my favorite foods, a spring treat that often makes a full meal. An artichoke is also a lovely appetizer, including at special dinner parties, when it can serve to relax guests who may not all know each other. It's hard to remain strangers when you're all nibbling something so delicious with your fingers.

4 large artichokes, preferably Green Globe variety, trimmed
2 or 3 garlic cloves, peeled and thinly sliced
1 tablespoon olive oil
Kosher salt
Mustard Mayonnaise, page 48

Set the artichokes on a clean work surface and cut the stems even with the body of the artichoke, so that it stands upright.

Turn the artichoke on its side, hold it still with your nondominant hand, and use a sharp knife to cut off about one inch of its tip. When all of the artichokes have been cut, set them upright and push slivers of garlic here and there among the leaves. Drizzle a little olive oil into the center of each one.

Put the artichokes into a deep saucepan that will hold them tightly. Add a tablespoon or so of salt and add enough water to cover the artichokes.

Bring to a boil over high heat, reduce the heat, and simmer gently, covered, for 20 minutes. Uncover and use tongs to try to remove a leaf. If it comes out with just a bit of resistance, the artichokes are done. If not, continue to cook and test every 5 minutes. Do not overcook.

Remove from the water and let drain for a few minutes.

While the artichokes cook, make the Mustard Mayonnaise.

Serve hot, at room temperature, or chilled, with the Mustard Mayonnaise alongside.

Variations:

- Serve with Mustard Cream (page 221) instead of Mustard Mayonnaise.

- Drizzle a tablespoon or two of Mustard Vinaigrette (page 226) before serving warm with Mustard Cream (page 221).

NOTE

To make Mustard Mayonnaise to serve four, put 6 tablespoons best-quality mayonnaise into a small bowl, add 2 tablespoons extra-strong Dijon mustard or any favorite mustard, stir, taste and correct for salt, if needed. Cover and chill until ready to serve.

Roasted Asparagus
with Prosciutto and Mustard

Serves 4 to 6

Asparagus spears wrapped in prosciutto became very popular in the late 1980s and early 1990s but it was often disappointing, primarily because of how the asparagus was cooked. Steamed or boiled, asparagus becomes a bit stringy and dilute. If you roast in a hot oven, its flavors and textures are concentrated and utterly delicious; asparagus cooked in this way needs no peeling and will not become stringy. As far as size goes, bigger is better. There is a mistaken perception that the thinnest spears of asparagus are the youngest and thus the most flavorful. The opposite is actually true; the fattest spears are the ones a plant first puts out. Over the years, stalks become smaller and smaller.

1 pound fat asparagus stalks, tough
    ends snapped off
Olive oil
Kosher salt
Black pepper in a mill
½ pound very thinly sliced prosciutto
Dijon mustard
Fresh mustard flowers, if available

Preheat the oven to 450 degrees.

Put the asparagus on a baking sheet and drizzle with a very small amount of olive oil; using your hands, turn the spears to coat them. Season with salt and pepper, set on the middle rack of the oven and cook until tender, from 9 to 14 or so minutes, depending on their size.

Remove from the oven.

While the asparagus cooks, brush each slice of prosciutto very lightly with mustard. Put a tablespoon or so of mustard into a small serving bowl.

When the asparagus is still quite warm but has cooled enough to touch, wrap each spear in a piece of prosciutto and set it in a serving platter. Season all over the black pepper, add the bowl of mustard, garnish with mustard flowers, if available, and serve right away.

New Potatoes
with Mustard Butter and Mustard Cream

Serves 6 to 10 as an appetizer

This is one of those dishes that doesn't really need a full recipe but just a description. Little potatoes, just enough for a single mouthful, make excellent appetizers and I've noticed they are particularly welcome at memorial services and at the gatherings that often follow funerals. Even when grief has eclipsed your appetizer, the warm familiarity of a little potato beckons and offers a delicious nibble of both nourishment and comfort.

Oven-Roasted New Potatoes with Mustard Butter, page 220
Mustard Cream, page 221

Prepare the potatoes, using the tiniest ones you can find.

While the potatoes cook, make the mustard cream, put it in a serving bowl, cover, and refrigerate.

When the potatoes are done, put them in a serving bowl and serve hot, with the sauce and plenty of toothpicks alongside.

Beet Caviar
with Egg Mimosa, Créme Fraiche & Croutons
Serves 6 to 8

Beet caviar gets its name from its small dice, almost as tiny as fish eggs. Here, I pair it with condiments we enjoy with true caviar, egg, chives, and créme fraiche. Both vinegar and mustard are natural companions to beets, as they mitigate some of the root's stronger flavors. Try this with a favorite flavored mustard. Blue Cheese and White Wine Mustard from Maille, and Walnut Mustard, Tarragon Mustard, and Black Currant Mustard from Edmond Fallot are delightful with minced beets.

1 bunch (about 1½ pounds) red
    beets, trimmed, and roasted
    (see Note below)
1 small red onion, trimmed and
    peeled
2 tablespoons minced fresh parsley
2 tablespoons best-quality red
    wine vinegar
1 tablespoon Dijon mustard, plus
    more to taste

Kosher salt
Black pepper in a mill
3 tablespoons extra virgin olive oil
8 ounces créme fraiche
1 baguette, sliced diagonally and
    lightly toasted
1 hard-cooked farm egg, peeled
    and grated
1 teaspoon fresh snipped chives

Roast the beets and let them cool.

Meanwhile, cut the onion into 1/8-inch dice and put it into a medium bowl. Add the parsley, vinegar and mustard, toss and season with salt and pepper. Set aside.

When the beets have cooled, use your fingers to peel them. Using a very sharp knife, cut them into 1/8-inch dice. Add to the onion mixture, toss, add the olive oil, taste and correct for mustard, salt and pepper. Transfer to a small serving bowl and set on a large platter.

Spread créme fraiche over the toasted bread and set on the platter.

Working quickly, toss together the egg and chives, season with salt and pepper and scatter over the beets.

Serve right away, with a small spoon so guests may top the croutons with some of the beet caviar.

NOTE
To roast beets, trim off their stems and set them on a sheet of aluminum foil. Add enough olive oil to lubricate them, fold the foil over the beets, seal the edges and set on a baking sheet in a 375 degree oven. Bake for 45 to 50 minutes or a bit longer for medium to large beets. Remove from the oven.

Rock Shrimp
with Remoulade Sauce

Serves 4 to 6

Rock shrimp have a delicate, sweet flavor that I love, though this dish is equally delicious made with other wild shrimp. For both environmental and health concerns, I do not recommend farmed shrimp or prawns.

½ cup Remoulade Sauce, page 225
1 pound rock shrimp or unshelled medium prawns
Olive oil
Kosher salt
Black pepper in a mill
1 lemon
1 fennel bulb, trimmed and every thinly sliced
1 bunch radishes, trimmed and quartered
1 pint small strawberries, optional
Fresh Italian parsley sprigs, for garnish

First, make the sauce; this can be done up to 2 days in advance.

Shortly before serving, prepare the rock shrimp. Pour a little olive oil into a heavy skillet set over high heat, add the shrimp, and sauté, turning or tossing nearly continuously, until they turn pink, about 2 to 3 minutes. Do not overcook.

Working quickly, transfer to a bowl, season with salt and pepper, and squeeze lemon juice over them. Set aside.

Put the sauce into a small bowl, set it in the center of a serving platter, and spread the fennel around it. Scatter the shrimp on top of the fennel. Add strawberries here and there, if using, and garnish with radishes and parsley sprigs.

Serve right away.

Root Vegetable Remoulade
with Smoked Salmon

Serves 6 to 8

Sometimes I start Thanksgiving dinner with a favorite fall soup or with fresh cracked crab, but this starter, paired with smoked fish or not, is wonderful, too, especially with a chilled Brut Rosé alongside. This sauce is not identical to the Remoulade on page 225 but it is very easy to prepare.

1 small to medium celery root, peeled and trimmed
2 medium carrots, peeled and trimmed
2 parsnips, peeled and trimmed
1 bunch radishes, trimmed
Juice of 1 lemon
1 cup crème fraîche or a blend of ½ cup crème fraîche and ½ cup
  mayonnaise
⅓ cup Dijon mustard
1 tablespoon brined green peppercorns, optional
2 tablespoon fresh snipped chives
Kosher salt
Black pepper in a mill
10 to 12 ounces gravlax, smoked salmon, smoked trout, smoked sturgeon, or
  other smoked fish

Using the large blade of a box grater or the large grating blade of a food processor, grate the vegetables and transfer them to a medium mixing bowl. If you prefer, use a mandoline's narrow blade to cut the vegetables into small julienne. Add the lemon juice and toss well. Set aside briefly.

Put the crème fraîche (and mayonnaise, if using) and mustard into a small bowl and stir until smooth. Add the green peppercorns, if using, and the chives, taste, and season with salt and pepper. Set aside about ⅓ cup of the dressing, add the rest to the bowl with the grated vegetables. Toss gently but thoroughly. Taste and adjust for salt and pepper as needed.

Cover and refrigerate until ready to serve.

To serve, divide the remoulade among individual plates and top with some of the smoked fish. Add a dollop of the reserved dressing and serve right away.

Soups

In the United States, we don't see a lot of soups in which mustard is a main ingredient, but they have been common throughout history, especially in northern Europe. In India, you find many variations of dal, a type of soup that calls for lentils or other legumes and frequently includes mustard seed in its spice mixture. A simple mustard cream, added moments before serving, is an easy and delicious way to add the pleasing bite of mustard to bean soups and split pea soups.

Split Pea Soup with Mustard Cream
Bacon and Mustard Soup
Cream of Mustard Soup with Four Variations
Mustard Vichyssoise with Fresh Dungeness Crab
Mustard Greens Soup with Mustard Yogurt Sauce
Squash Broth with Mustard Greens and White Beans
Channa Dal with Rice, Yogurt & Chutney

Split Pea Soup
with Mustard Cream

Serves 6 to 8

Almost everyone loves a good split pea soup, especially one made from scratch. The soup is sweet from the peas and smoky and salty from the ham hocks, making a swirl of mustard the perfect complement.

2 tablespoons olive oil
2 tablespoons butter
2 leeks, white and pale green parts
    only, thoroughly washed and
    thinly sliced
1 yellow onion, trimmed and cut
    into small dice
2 carrots, trimmed, peeled, and cut
    into small dice
4 to 5 garlic cloves, minced

Kosher salt
6 cups homemade chicken stock or
    vegetable stock
2 ham hocks
1 bay leaf
1 pound split peas, picked over for
    rocks, etc., soaked overnight
Black pepper in a mill
⅓ cup Rainwater Madeira, optional
½ cup Mustard Cream, page 221

Pour the olive oil into a large soup pot set over medium-low heat, add the butter, and when it is melted, add the leeks and onion. Cook gently until soft and fragrant, about 7 minutes. Do not let brown. Add the carrots, cook 5 minutes more, stir in the garlic, and cook another 2 minutes. Season fairly generously with salt.

Stir in the stock, add 2 cups of water, and add the ham hocks and bay leaf. Increase the heat to high, bring to a boil, and then return the heat to low. Simmer gently for 1½ hours, until the meat is nearly falling off the bone.

Drain the split peas, stir them into the pot, and cook gently until they begin to fall apart, about 45 minutes. Use tongs to transfer the ham hocks to a bowl or plate and remove and discard the bay leaves.

Use an immersion blender to puree the soup.

Let the meat cool slightly, pull it off the bone, and stir it into the pot, along with the Madeira, if using. Season with black pepper, taste, and correct for salt. Cover, remove from the heat, and let rest for about 10 minutes.

Ladle into soup bowls or soup plates, top each portion with a generous swirl of mustard cream, and serve right away.

Bacon and Mustard Soup

Serves 6 to 8

   This soup is inspired by the mustard soups of the Netherlands, where there were once scores of small grocers who made their own mustard. Most of those producers have faded into history, but one, Abraham's Groningen Mustard Factory, remains. It is located in a small village in Eenrum, a short drive from Groningen, and includes a museum and a restaurant. They may be best known for their mustard soup, which has inspired many versions, including several with bacon.

8 ounces thick bacon, cut into
   ¼-inch wide crosswise strips
2 tablespoons butter
½ cup all-purpose flour
2 shallots, minced
5 cups homemade chicken
   stock, hot
2 tablespoons coarse-grain mustard,
   preferably Groningen's

2 tablespoons smooth mustard,
   preferably Groningen's, or Dijon
   mustard
¾ cup heavy cream
4 ounces Gouda or similar cheese,
   grated
Black pepper in a mill
Kosher salt
2 tablespoons snipped fresh chives

Fry the bacon in a large soup pot or Dutch oven until it is crisp. Use a slotted spoon to transfer it to absorbent paper to drain. Pour off all but 2 tablespoons of the fat, return the pan to medium heat, and add the butter. When the butter is completely melted, add the flour and whisk constantly until the mixture turns a golden brown. *Do not let it burn.*

Add the shallots and continue to whisk for 2 to 3 minutes. Slowly pour in the stock, whisking all the while, and let simmer for about 5 minutes. Whisk in both mustards and the cream. Heat through but do not bring to a boil, stir in the cheese, season with several very generous turns of black pepper, and remove from the heat. Taste and correct for salt.

To serve, divide the soup among individual bowls and top with bacon and chives.

Enjoy right away.

Cream of Mustard Soup
with Four Variations

Serves 6

Consider this soup a master recipe. It is quite good on its own but even better when it forms a canvas for other foods. Its roots are deep, with versions found in some of the earliest French cookbooks. This version is my own but inspired on the traditional recipe. I added aromatics, which are so readily available to us today. My favorite additions follow the main recipe.

6 tablespoons butter
1 leek, white part only, thinly sliced
1 small yellow onion, chopped
1 small carrot, peeled and thinly
    sliced
1 shallot, minced
3 cloves garlic, minced
6 tablespoons all-purpose flour
Kosher salt
3 cups homemade chicken stock,
    heated

1½ cups half-and-half or milk,
    scalded
1 small bouquet garni (fresh oregano,
    thyme, Italian parsley, marjoram)
½ cup heavy cream
2 egg yolks, beaten
¼ cup Dijon mustard
White pepper
Salt
1 tablespoon snipped fresh chives

Put the butter into a soup pot set over medium-low heat and, when it is melted, add the leek, onion, carrot, and shallot. Sauté gently until they are soft and fragrant, about 10 to 12 minutes; do not let them brown. Add the garlic and sauté 2 minutes more. Whisk in the flour and cook, stirring continuously, for 5 minutes. Season with salt.

Whisk in the chicken stock and the half-and-half or milk, add the bouquet garni, and simmer, gently and uncovered, for about 30 to 35 minutes.

Strain the liquid into a clean saucepan, add the cream, and bring almost to a boil. Reduce the heat to low.

Use a small ladle to add a bit of the soup to the egg yolks, whisking all the while; add a bit more, whisk, and add a bit more again. When the egg yolks are quite warm, slowly whisk the mixture into the soup. Heat thoroughly but do not let boil. Remove from the heat, whisk in the mustard, and season with several turns of pepper. Taste and correct for salt.

To serve, ladle into soup plates, garnish with chives, and serve right away.

Variations:
- Steam about 2 cups of broccoli or cauliflower florets until just tender, add them to each bowl of soup, and serve.

- Top each soup with several pieces of roasted asparagus, season generously with black pepper, and serve.

- Warm about 12 ounces of shredded cooked chicken, preferably thigh meat, and divide it among the soup plates, ladle the soup over it, garnish with chives, and serve.

- Sauté 6 sea scallops or 12 ounces calico scallops in brown butter for 90 seconds, turn and cook for 90 seconds more. Season with salt and pepper and add one to each soup plate after adding the soup. Garnish with chives and serve.

Mustard Vichyssoise
with Fresh Dungeness Crab

Serve 4 to 6

This suave soup is a favorite winter holiday dish, as Dungeness crab season usually opens in Northern California, where I live, just in time for Thanksgiving. It is a lovely first course for any dinner party. Use whatever crab you have, adjusting the quantities and seasoning accordingly.

3 tablespoons butter

4 leeks, white and palest green parts only, thoroughly cleaned and sliced into thin rounds

1 small yellow onion, peeled and diced

Kosher salt

2 pounds (about 3 to 4 large) potatoes, peeled and very thinly sliced

3 cups homemade chicken stock or fish fumet

Grated zest of 1 lemon

2 tablespoons Dijon mustard

½ cup crème fraîche, plus more to taste

White pepper in a mill

1¼ pound fresh cooked crab meat (meat from 1 small to medium dungeness crab), leg meat reserved separately, chilled

2 teaspoons minced lemon zest

2 tablespoons mustard oil or best-quality extra virgin olive oil

1 tablespoon fresh snipped chives

Melt the butter in a large heavy pot set over medium-low heat and when it is foamy, add the leeks and saute until they are wilted, about 7 to 8 minutes. Add the onion and continue to cook until the onions soften and become fragrant, about 12 minutes more. Season with salt.

Add the potatoes, sauté 2 minutes, add the stock or fumet and 3 cups of water, increase the heat to high, and when the liquid boils, reduce the heat and simmer gently until the potatoes are tender, about 15 minutes. Remove from the heat and let rest about 10 minutes.

Puree the soup using an immersion blender or a food mill and strain through a fine sieve into a large bowl. Stir in the lemon zest and mustard, cover, and refrigerate until thoroughly chilled, about 3 hours.

Chill individual soup plates.

To finish and serve the soup, remove it from the refrigerator. Stir the crème fraîche into the soup and season with several turns of white pepper, taste, and correct for salt. If you prefer the soup a bit richer, add another 2 or 3 tablespoons of crème fraîche.

Set the chilled soup plates on your work surface and divide the chilled body meat of the crab among them. Ladle soup over each portion of crab and agitate each plate briefly to distribute the soup evenly. Garnish each portion with 1 or 2 pieces of leg meat, drizzle with a little oil, and sprinkle with chives.

Serve right away.

Mustard Greens Soup
with Mustard Yogurt Sauce

Serves 6 to 8

Potatoes are an excellent base for a wide array of soups; they provide an earthy canvas and voluptuous texture that enhances rather than eclipses other flavors, as cream often does. In this soup, spinach and parsley contribute both flavor and color.

3 tablespoons olive oil
1 yellow onion, minced
1 small carrot, peeled and minced
6 garlic cloves, minced
Kosher salt
Black pepper in a mill
3 pounds potatoes, scrubbed and
    thinly sliced
2 to 3 cups chicken stock

1 bunch mustard greens, large stems
    trimmed and discard
Olive oil
2 generous handfuls of young spinach
    leaves
1 cup, loosely packed Italian parsley
    leaves, chopped
Mustard Yogurt Sauce, page 223

Heat the olive oil in a large pot set over medium heat. Add the onions and carrots, lower the heat, and sauté until the vegetables are tender and fragrant, about 15 minutes. Stir now and then to prevent them from sticking to the bottom of the pan. Add half the garlic and sauté two minutes more. Season with salt and pepper. Add the potatoes to the pot, stir, add the chicken stock and enough water to completely cover the potatoes by about 2 inches.

Increase the heat, bring the liquid to a boil, lower the heat, and simmer, partially covered, until the potatoes are tender, about 20 minutes.

While the potatoes cook, prepare the greens. Set the mustard greens on a clean work surface and cut them into half-inch crosswise slices.

Pour a little olive oil into a large sauté pan set over medium heat, add the mustard greens, and cook, turning gently, until they begin to wilt. When they are almost fully wilted, add the spinach and cook 2 minutes more. Add the remaining garlic and the parsley, turn two or three times, and remove from the heat.

When the potatoes are almost tender, add the greens and cook 5 minutes more, or until both the greens and the potatoes are tender.

Remove from the heat, taste, and correct for salt and pepper.

Serve right away or puree with an immersion blender first. Ladle into soup bowls, add a very generous spoonful of the sauce, and serve.

Squash Broth
with Mustard Greens and White Beans

Serves 4

A broth of winter squash reveals the sweet essence of this hearty vegetable, with a flavor that is both intense and delicate; it is a perfect counterpoint to the pleasing bitterness of the greens and the creaminess of the white beans.

1 winter squash, 5 to 6 pounds, preferably butternut, acorn, or a similar variety, cut into pieces, seeds removed
2 medium or 1 large leek, white and green parts, carefully washed and sliced
4 cups sliced mustard greens
Kosher salt
Black pepper in a mill
1 cup cannellini beans, soaked overnight, drained, and cooked in simmering water until tender
2 tablespoons chopped cilantro leaves
½ teaspoon cumin seed, toasted

Preheat the oven to 325 degrees.

Set the squash on a baking sheet, brush the cut parts of the squash with a bit of olive oil, and bake until tender, about 45 minutes. Remove from the oven, cool slightly, and peel.

Put the peeled squash into a large soup pot, add the sliced leeks, and pour in about 12 to 16 cups of water. Slowly bring to a boil over medium heat, reduce the heat to low, and simmer very gently for about 2 hours.

Line a large strainer or colander with cheesecloth and strain the liquid into a clean pot. Set over medium heat and simmer until it is reduced to just 6 cups.

The broth can be held at this point for 2 to 3 days.

To finish the soup, heat the broth. Pour a little olive oil into a saute pan set over medium heat, add the greens, and sauté, turning frequently, until just tender. Season with salt and pepper.

Add the greens and the beans to the stock and heat through.

Ladle into soup plates, garnish with cilantro leaves and cumin seed, and serve right away.

Channa Dal

with Rice, Yogurt & Chutney

Serves 4 to 8

In the mid-seventies, I spent a few months in India and came to love the simple foods of the countryside where I stayed. My meals were made up primarily of sliced cucumbers and tomatoes, a pomegranate, a big bowl of rice, and a simple soup of either channa dal (yellow split peas) or masoor dal (red lentils) spooned over the rice. This is my own version, the one I've been making since my return from that remarkable adventure. If this is part of a larger meal, it will serve as many as eight; as a main course, it will serve up to four.

1 cup channa dal (split baby chickpeas), red lentils, or yellow split peas, picked through and soaked in water for several hours or overnight
3 tablespoons clarified butter or olive oil
1 yellow onion, cut into small dice
3 or 4 cloves garlic, minced
Kosher salt
1 teaspoon white mustard seeds
1 teaspoon brown mustard seeds
1 teaspoon ground cumin
1 teaspoon ground turmeric
½ teaspoon ground cayenne, plus more to taste
½ teaspoon ground cardamom
Whole nutmeg
1 tablespoon freshly grated ginger
1 cup basmati or jasmine rice, rinsed
Black pepper in a mill
¾ cup plain whole milk yogurt
Onion Chutney or other chutney of choice
½ cup plain yogurt
½ cup chopped fresh cilantro leaves

Drain the lentils, put them into a medium saucepan, and add about 4 cups of water. Bring to a boil over high heat, reduce the heat, and simmer gently until the lentils soften and begin to fall apart. Add water as needed. Skim off any foam that forms on the surface.

Meanwhile, put the clarified butter or olive oil into a medium sauté pan set over medium low heat, add the onion, and sauté until soft and fragrant, about 10 to 12 minutes. Add the garlic, sauté 2 minutes more, and season with salt.

Add the mustard seeds, cumin, turmeric, cayenne, cardamom, and a few gratings of nutmeg. Stir gently for 2 minutes. Add the grated ginger, stir, and remove from the heat.

Cook the rice according to package directions; remove from the heat and let rest 10 to 15 minutes before fluffing with a fork.

When the lentils are nearly tender, stir in the onion mixture and continue to cook gently until the lentils have completely fallen apart; thin with a little water if necessary to achieve a proper soup texture, which should be thick but not too thick. Taste, correct for salt, and season with several generous turns of black pepper.

To serve, add a scoop of rice to individual bowls and ladle soup over it. Add a dollop of yogurt, a spoonful of chutney, and cilantro leaves, and serve right away.

Variation:
- Sauté 1 bunch of mustard greens, trimmed and sliced, in a little butter or olive oil until tender, season with salt, and stir into the dal just before serving it.

Salads

So many salads rely on mustard, some in which mustard is a forward flavor and others in which it plays a supporting role, a complementary bass line to the main ingredients' melody. In both instances, mustard is essential.

The dishes in this chapter are, for the most part, mine, a result of simply cooking through the seasons, year after year. Just one, Celeri Remoulade, comes from the world's culinary canon.

To make the very best salads, you must use fresh pert greens and other ingredients at their peak of flavor, though there is more margin of error when it comes to root vegetables and legumes than with fresh vegetables. If you can grow lettuces, herbs, radishes, kales, and such in your own garden, you're already set. If you can't and have not been happy with supermarket options, find a farmers' market near you. If a farmers' market is not an option, buy whole lettuces, whole cabbages, whole carrots, and such, not the kind that have been washed, trimmed and packed into sealed bags. You get more for your money, fresher ingredients, and more control over quantity.

Creamy Coleslaw

Cole Slaw with Ginger, Mustard & Sesame Seeds

All-American Macaroni Salad

Summer Potato Salad with Radishes & Green Beans

Potato Salad with Italian Salami, Olives, Burrata & Arugula

Bread & Sausage Salad

Mustard Sprout & Farro Salad

Raw Kale Salad with Avocado, Tomatoes, Garlic & Lemon

Céleri Remoulade

Celery Root with Black Olives, Mustard & Crème Fraîche

Pasta Flan Salad with Romaine Lettuce & Caesar-Style Dressing

Composed Chicken and Pasta Salad with Caper-Dijon Dressing

Chickpea Salad with Mustard-Anchovy Vinaigrette

Warm Cabbage Salad with Goat Cheese, Spicy Toasted Pecans
& Maple-Mustard Dressing

Warm Leek, Potato, & Artichoke Salad with Mustard Vinaigrette

Creamy Coleslaw

Serves 6 to 8

Depending on where you live, you may prefer your coleslaw sweet or savory. If you like it sweet, use a sweet mustard instead of adding sugar.

2 tablespoons best-quality red wine vinegar, plus more to taste
½ cup sour cream
½ cup mayonnaise, preferably Best Foods/Hellman's brand
2 tablespoons coarse-grain mustard or other mustard of choice
Kosher salt
Black pepper in a mill

Tabasco sauce, optional
1 small red or green cabbage, cored and very thinly sliced
1 small red onion, cut into very thin rounds
2 carrots, trimmed, peeled, and grated
3 tablespoons finely chopped fresh Italian parsley

Put the vinegar, sour cream, mayonnaise, and mustard into a medium mixing bowl and whisk well. Taste, season with salt and pepper, and correct as needed for acid. Add a few shakes of Tabasco if you like a bit of heat and mix thoroughly.

Add the cabbage to the bowl.

Cut the sliced onions in half and add to the bowl, along with the carrots. Toss well, add the parsley, and toss again.

Serve right away or cover and refrigerate; remove from the refrigerator about 20 minutes before serving.

Cole Slaw

with Ginger, Mustard & Sesame Seeds

Serves 6 to 8

There are countless variations of cole slaw, some made with mayonnaise-based dressings, others, such as this one, with vinaigrette.

1 small green cabbage, cored and cut into very thin slices
2 carrots, peeled and grated
1 small red onion, cut into small dice
2 tablespoons apple cider vinegar
Juice of 1 lemon, about 3 tablespoons
3 tablespoons honey mustard of choice
2 garlic cloves, minced
1 tablespoon grated fresh ginger
Kosher salt
Black pepper in a mill
½ cup extra virgin olive oil
2 tablespoons toasted sesame oil
½ cup chopped fresh cilantro leaves
2 tablespoons white sesame seeds, lightly toasted

Put the cabbage, carrots, and onion into a medium serving bowl and toss together.

In a small bowl, whisk together the vinegar, lemon juice, and mustard and honey. Add the garlic and ginger, season with salt and pepper, taste, and correct for salt and acid. Whisk in the oils.

Pour the dressing over the vegetables and toss thoroughly. Add the cilantro and toss again.

Scatter the sesame seeds over the top and serve right away.

All-American Macaroni Salad

Serves 6 to 8

Sometimes this macaroni salad is just the thing, especially on a hot day when hot dogs and sausages are on the grill and there's fresh watermelon for dessert. Through all of the inventive pasta salads of the last several decades, this classic—so simple, so familiar—has endured. For an all-American potato salad, see the variation at the end of the main recipe.

1 pound small-shaped pasta, such as elbow, ditalini or tubetti
Kosher salt
1 cup mayonnaise, preferably Best Foods/Hellman's brand
3 tablespoons prepared mustard of choice (see note on next page)
2 tablespoons fresh lemon juice or white wine vinegar, plus more to taste
Black pepper in a mill
1 small red onion, cut into small dice
3 celery stalks, cut into small dice
⅓ cup sliced California-style black olives
3 tablespoons chopped fresh Italian parsley

Fill a large pot two-thirds full with water, add a very generous tablespoon of salt, and bring to a boil over high heat. Add the pasta and stir with a wooden spoon until the water returns to a boil. Cook according to package directions until just done. Drain, rinse, and tip into a wide shallow bowl.

While the pasta cooks, put the mayonnaise into a small bowl, add the mustard and lemon juice or white wine vinegar, and whisk together until smooth. Taste, correct for acid, and season with salt and several turns of black pepper.

Add the onion, celery, and olives to the drained pasta and toss gently. Fold in the dressing, add the parsley, and either serve right away or cover and refrigerate until ready to serve.

NOTE

The easiest way to vary the flavors of this dish is with the mustard. For something reminiscent of childhood picnics, use an American mustard, such as French's. For a more suave flavor, use Dijon, Pommery, or another French mustard. If you like your macaroni salad a bit sweet, use a honey mustard.

Variation:
- Make a traditional potato salad using this exact recipe. Just replace the pasta with 2 pounds of potatoes, sliced or cubed, and cooked until tender. Add 2 or 3 chopped hard-boiled eggs to the salad along with the olives.

Summer Potato Salad
with Radishes & Green Beans

Serves 6

I find the addition of radishes and green beans to this salad very refreshing. Tiny haricots verts are wonderful and it is worth the effort it takes to find them (or grow them, if you are blessed with garden space).

2 pounds small new potatoes, scrubbed but not peeled
Kosher salt
Mustard Vinaigrette, page 226
¾ pound Blue Lake green beans or haricots verts, trimmed
1 bunch radishes, trimmed and cut into very thin rounds
1 bunch green onions, trimmed and cut into very thin rounds
Black pepper in a mill
4 hard-boiled eggs, sliced
3 tablespoons chopped fresh Italian parsley

Cut the potatoes in half or in quarters, depending on their size. Put them into a large saucepan, add water to cover them by at least 2 inches, and season generously with salt. Bring to a boil over high heat, reduce the heat, and simmer gently until tender, about 20 minutes. Use a slotted spoon to transfer the potatoes to a colander to drain. Tip them into a wide shallow bowl, add half the vinaigrette, toss, and set aside.

Cut Blue Lake green beans into 1½ inch lengths (leave haricots verts whole) and carefully tip them into the cooking water. Simmer until tender, about 4 minutes for larger beans, 90 seconds for little ones. Test to be sure they are done. Drain and add to the potatoes, along with the radishes and onions.

Toss very gently, taste, and season with salt and pepper. Add the remaining dressing, toss gently, and fold in the eggs.

Sprinkle the Italian parsley on top and serve.

Variations:

- Cook 6 eggs. Slice 2 of them and cut 4 in half lengthwise. Fold the sliced eggs into the salad and set the halved eggs on top. Add a dollop of Mustard Cream, page 221, on top of each egg, grind black pepper over everything, sprinkle with Italian parsley, and serve.

- Cook 4 sausages of choice (sometimes I use bockwurst; sometimes I use Italian sausage), cut them into ¼-inch diagonal slices, and add to the salad along with the radishes and onions. Continue as directed in the main recipe.

Potato Salad
with Italian Salami, Olives, Burrata & Arugula

Serves 6

When I was first making this salad, I sometimes added mozzarella fresca to it. That was before burrata was available in the US. Now that it is, I use it instead. If you prefer mozzarella fresca, tear it or cut it into pieces and add it to the salad at the last minute, just before tipping it onto the arugula.

2 pounds very small new red potatoes, scrubbed, halved, and cooked in salted water until tender, drained
1 tablespoon red wine vinegar
Juice of 1 lemon
2 tablespoons Dijon mustard or other mustard of choice

Kosher salt
Black pepper in a mill
½ cup extra virgin olive oil
8 ounces Italian salami, such as soppressata, thinly sliced
¾ cup pitted Niçoise olives
2 bunches arugula
8 ounces (1 piece) burrata

Put the potatoes into a wide, shallow bowl.

In a small bowl, combine the vinegar, lemon juice, and mustard, season with salt and pepper. Whisk in the olive oil, toss, and correct the seasoning. Pour half the dressing over the potatoes and toss gently.

Add the salami and olives and toss gently.

Spread the arugula over a platter and set the burrata in the center. Mound the salad all around the cheese, drizzle with the remaining dressing, and grind black pepper over everything.

Serve right away.

Bread & Sausage Salad

Serves 6 to 8

The most important rule for bread salad is to use the best bread you can find, a sturdy hearth bread that won't break down in the dressing. It is a great way to use up good-quality leftovers (roasted chicken, for example) or too many garden vegetables at harvest. This version echoes one of life's simplest culinary pleasures, good sausage in great bread slathered with mustard. This dish captures that rustic spirit in a salad that is both delicious and portable, an easy thing to take along to the beach, park, or hiking trail. If you plan to transport it, keep the sliced sausages in a separate container that will keep them warm, and add them just before eating.

6 cups day-old hearth bread torn into 1-inch pieces
Mustard Vinaigrette, page 226
1 pound sausages of choice
1 small red onion, cut into small dice
4 garlic cloves, minced
1 tablespoon yellow mustard seeds
Kosher salt
Black pepper in a mill
3 tablespoons chopped fresh Italian parsley

Toss the bread with half the vinaigrette and let sit for 30 minutes.

Broil, grill, or fry the sausages until done, and drain on absorbent paper. Cut into small rounds and add to the bread, along with the onion, garlic, and mustard seeds. Toss, add the remaining dressing, toss again, taste, and correct for salt. Season with several turns of black pepper, add the parsley, toss, and serve right away.

Mustard Sprout & Farro Salad

Serves 6 to 8

Mustard sprouts are easy to grow at home and are quite delicious, with a bright mustardy flavor and a bit of heat. If you don't want to wait the three to four days it takes to grow the sprouts, you can make this salad using radish sprouts or onion sprouts, both of which are sometimes available at farmers' markets.

2 cups farro
Kosher salt
Juice of 2 lemons, plus more as needed
1 bunch (8 to 10) radishes, preferably French Breakfast variety, trimmed
3 scallions, white and green parts, very thinly sliced
8 ounces Bulgarian or French feta, drained and crumbled
5 tablespoons extra virgin olive oil, plus more as needed
Black pepper in a mill
1 cup mustard sprouts, page 275

Put the farro into a strainer, rinse under cool running water, and transfer to a medium saucepan. Add water to cover plus 3 inches, stir in 3 tablespoons kosher salt, and bring to a boil over high heat. Skim off any foam that forms on top. Reduce the heat to medium-low and simmer until the farro is tender but toothsome, about 35 to 45 minutes.

Drain, transfer to a wide shallow serving bowl, drizzle with lemon juice, and let cool for 15 minutes. Cover with a tea towel for up to 2 hours.

To finish the salad, shave the radishes as thinly as possible and add them to the bowl of farro, along with the scallions and crumbled feta. Drizzle the olive oil and toss gently. Taste for acid balance, adding a bit more lemon if it is not tart enough or a bit more olive oil if it is too tart. Correct for salt and season with several generous turns of black pepper. Add the mustard sprouts, toss a time or two, and serve right away.

Raw Kale Salad
with Avocado, Tomatoes, Garlic & Lemon

Serves 3 to 4

In recent years, kale has been the bran muffin of the decade, the magic food bullet that will keep you thin, cancer-free, and almost immortal. Raw kale salads have been particularly possible—cooking food destroys its nutrients, doncha know—and while some are good many present quite a challenge. It is important to let a salad of raw kale rest after dressing it.

1 bunch Lacinato kale, rinsed, dried,
    central stems removed
Kosher salt
3 garlic cloves, pressed
Red pepper flakes
2 tablespoons coarse-grain mustard
6 tablespoons best-quality extra
    virgin olive oil

Juice of 1 lemon
1 firm ripe avocado, cubed
2 cups small cherry tomatoes,
    preferably yellow and orange, cut
    in half
Black pepper in a mill

Stack several leaves, roll them tightly lengthwise, and cut into ⅛-inch wide crosswise slices. Continue until all the leaves have been cut. Put the leaves into a deep bowl, season with salt, and use your fingers to separate and fluff the leaves, rubbing in the salt as you do. Add half the garlic, a pinch of red pepper flakes, the mustard, half the olive oil, and half the lemon juice, toss and set aside for about 30 minutes.

Meanwhile, put the avocado and tomatoes into a bowl, season lightly with salt, and add the remaining garlic, olive oil and lemon juice. Taste, correct for salt, and season with several turns of black pepper. Cover and set aside.

To finish the salad, toss the kale, taste a piece, and adjust the seasoning, if needed. Divide it among individual plates or bowls and top with some of the avocado-tomato mixture. Serve immediately.

Variation:
- To enjoy this salad when tomatoes are not in season, simply omit them and use 2 avocados instead of just one.

Céleri Remoulade

Serves 4 to 6

Celery root, sometimes called celeriac, is a wonderful vegetable, with an earthy flavor that pairs beautifully with a smooth Dijon mustard, including in this classic French bistro dish.

½ cup crème fraîche
2 tablespoons Dijon mustard or Green Peppercorn Mustard
1 tablespoons fresh lemon juice, plus more to taste
Kosher salt
Black pepper in a mill
1 celery root, about 1¼ pounds

Put the crème fraîche and mustard into a medium bowl, add the lemon juice, and mix well. Taste, correct for acid, and season with salt and pepper.

Peel the celery root, cutting away any green and all the brown skin. Cut the bulb into quarters and grate on the large blade of a box grater or food processor. Add the grated celery root to the dressing and turn gently until uniformly mixed. Taste and correct for salt and pepper.

Serve right away.

Serving Suggestions: as an appetizer with gravlax or lox with mustard cream; as an appetizer with smoked trout or other smoked fish.

Celery Root
with Black Olives, Mustard & Crème Fraîche

Serves 4

Although celery root is delicious on its own, it also combines beautifully with other ingredients.

1 celery root, about 1¼ pounds, trimmed and cut into small julienne
Kosher salt
½ cup crème fraîche
2 to 3 tablespoons Olive Mustard, page 249

Black pepper in a mill
12 oil-cured black olives, pitted and minced
1 teaspoon fresh thyme leaves
Thyme sprigs, for garnish

Rinse the celery root in cool water and drain it thoroughly. Prepare an ice water bath in a medium bowl. Bring a large saucepan of salted water to a boil over high heat, add the celery root, and blanch for 2 to 3 minutes, until the root has just barely lost its raw crunch. Drain and cool in the ice water bath.

Drain the celery root thoroughly, put it in a bowl, cover, and chill until ready to serve.

In a small bowl, mix together the crème fraîche and mustard. Season to taste with salt and several turns of black pepper.

Toss the olives and thyme leaves with the celery root, add the dressing, and toss thoroughly. Divide among individual plates, garnish with thyme sprigs, and serve immediately.

Variation:
- Use half the amount of celery root and omit the olives. Cut 1 medium fennel bulb, 1 peeled and cored apple, and 1 bunch of radishes into small julienne. Dress with Honey-Pepper Mustard and serve on a bed of fresh watercress.

Pasta Flan Salad
with Romaine Lettuce & Caesar-Style Dressing

Serves 6 as a main course, 12 as a first course

This is perhaps my favorite recipe in the book. It is as dramatic on the plate as it is delicious on the palate, a sort of dressed-up tribute to Caesar salad. I particularly enjoy the way you can sense the texture of the thin strands of angel hair in the custard, as the anchovies, pancetta, cheese, and mustard work together in happy harmony. This salad is filling enough to be the centerpiece of a meal, with a light soup beforehand and fresh fruit afterwards. The custards can he made in advance, but should be brought to room temperature before serving.

For the custard:

¼ pound imported capellini (angel hair)

Kosher salt

Olive oil

3 ounces pancetta, cut into small dice and fried until almost crisp

2 cups whole milk

4 large pastured eggs, beaten in a medium bowl until light and thick

1 tablespoon Dijon mustard

Black pepper in a mill

6 ounces Parmigiano-Reggiano, grated on a medium blade

For the dressing:

3 anchovy fillets

3 cloves garlic

1 tablespoon Dijon mustard

1 egg yolk

Juice of 1 lemon, plus more to taste

⅔ cup extra virgin olive oil

¼ cup Parmigiano-Reggiano, grated

1 large or 2 small heads romaine lettuce, trimmed, rinsed, dried

Black pepper in a mill

Kosher salt

6 (or 12, if a first course) slices hearth bread, lightly grilled or toasted

A Mustard Cookbook

Preheat the oven to 350 degrees.

Fill a large saucepan half full with water, add 2 tablespoons kosher salt, and bring to a boil over high heat. When the water boils, add the pasta and stir until the water returns to a boil. Cook according to package directions until the pasta is just al dente. Drain the pasta, rinse it in cool water, and shake it to remove as much water as possible. Transfer to a wide shallow bowl to cool completely.

Meanwhile, brush a 12-cup muffin tin with olive oil. Divide the pancetta among the individual muffin cups.

Whisk the milk into the eggs, add the mustard and several generous turns of black pepper, and mix thoroughly.

Coil the pasta into the muffin cups, filling them about half full. Fill each cup with the custard mixture.

Carefully set the muffin tin on the middle rack of the oven and cook until puffed and lightly browned, about 25 minutes. Remove from the oven and let rest until easy to handle. Loosen each flan by running a thin knife around its circumference and then gently remove them. Invert onto a clean work surface.

While the flan cooks, prepare the dressing. To do so, put the anchovies and garlic into a suribachi and use a wooden pestle to crush and grind them into a thick paste. Add the egg yolk, lemon juice, and mustard and mix thoroughly. Use a whisk to mix in the olive oil a bit at a time. Fold in the cheese, add several turns of black pepper, taste, and correct for acid and salt, if needed. Set aside. (If you prefer, you can make the dressing in a food processor fitted with its metal blade.)

To serve, divide the lettuce among individual plates and season lightly with salt and pepper. Add flan—2 if a main course, 1 if a first course. Grill or toast the bread, brush it with a bit of olive oil, and season it with salt and pepper. Spoon a little dressing over each portion, add a slice of bread, and serve right away.

Composed Chicken and Pasta Salad
with Caper-Dijon Dressing

Serves 4 to 6 as a main course

One of my culinary students deserves credit for this dish. While I was working on the first edition of this book, she brought me a jar of her caper-anchovy dressing. With one taste, this salad sprang to mind, nearly fully formed. If you have a large glass salad bowl, make and present the salad in it, as it is both beautiful and dramatic.

Caper-Dijon Dressing, page 228
6 ounces spaghettini
Kosher salt
Juice of 1 lemon
1 tablespoon extra virgin olive oil
Black pepper in a mill
4 ounces pancetta or bacon, diced, cooked until just crisp, drained

3 cups cooked chicken, torn into shreds
1 head of Romaine lettuce, trimmed, cored, and torn into bite-sized pieces
2½ cups freshly made black pepper croutons (see note below)

Make the dressing and set it aside.

Fill a large saucepan half full with water, season with a generous 2 tablespoons of salt, and bring to a boil over high heat. When the water boils, add the spaghettini and stir until the water returns to a boil. Cook until it is just done, drain, and rinse with cool water. Shake off as much water as possible and transfer to a wide shallow bowl. Add the lemon juice and the olive oil, season with salt and pepper, toss gently, and set aside.

To assemble the salad, set a clean, clear glass salad bowl on a clean work surface, add half the lettuce, and season very lightly with salt. Top with half the pasta, followed by half the chicken and half the pancetta and bacon. Spoon half the dressing on top.

Build the second layer. Top with the croutons.

To serve, use two large serving forks inserted down into the salad to pull out each portion.

NOTE

To make the croutons, tear good hearth bread into bite-sized pieces. Put about ⅓ cup of extra virgin olive oil into a quart Mason jar, add several generous turns of black pepper, and add the bread. Secure the lid and shake the jar until the olive oil has been absorbed by the bread. Tip the bread out onto a baking sheet, set on the middle rack of a 250 degree oven, and toast, stirring now and then, until golden brown. Remove from the oven and let cool.

Chickpea Salad
with Mustard-Anchovy Vinaigrette

Serves 6 to 8

If you keep a well-stocked pantry, you can make this salad quite quickly, using canned chickpeas if need be. Just be sure to drain and rinse them first.

1 cup dried chickpeas, soaked in water overnight and simmered in salted water until tender, drained
Mustard-Anchovy Vinaigrette, page 227
Kosher salt
4 ounces small dried pasta, such as tripolini, ditalini, or small shells
1 cucumber, peeled, seeded, and cut into small dice

1 bunch radishes, trimmed and cut into small dice
3 green onions, trimmed and very thinly sliced
2 garlic cloves, minced
2 tablespoons minced Italian parsley
3 ounces feta cheese, crumbled

Make the vinaigrette and set it aside.

Fill a medium saucepan half full with water, add a tablespoon of salt, and bring to a boil over high heat. Add the pasta and stir until the water returns to a boil. Cooking according to package directions until the pasta is tender.

Meanwhile, put the chickpeas into a medium bowl, add the cucumber, radishes, onion, and garlic and toss gently. When the pasta is cooked, drain it, rinse it in cool water, shake off as much water as possible, and add it to the bowl.

Add the vinaigrette and toss gently.

Add the parsley and feta, toss again and serve at room temperature.

Variation:
• Add a can of best-quality tuna packed in olive oil and drained.

Warm Cabbage Salad
with Goat Cheese, Spicy Toasted Pecans & Maple-Mustard Dressing

Serves 4

Although good cabbage is available all year long, I prefer this sweet-and-savory salad in the winter, when its rich flavors and luscious textures are just the thing on a cold night.

1 teaspoon hot mustard flour or Colman's dry mustard
1 teaspoon water
1 small red cabbage, cored and very thinly sliced
8 ounces bacon, cooked until crisp and drained
½ cup extra virgin olive oil
2 cloves garlic, minced
3 tablespoons commercial Maple Mustard or a 1 tablespoon maple syrup,
    honey, or light molasses combined with 2 tablespoons Dijon mustard
3 tablespoons apple cider vinegar
Kosher salt
Black pepper in a mill
5 ounces chabis or other young, fresh chèvre
Spicy Toasted Pecans, page 212

Mix the mustard flour and cold water and set it aside for 20 minutes. Core and finely shred the cabbage and set it aside.

Cook the bacon until crisp and transfer it to absorbent paper to cool; reserve the drippings.

Meanwhile, whisk together the olive oil, 2 tablespoons of the pan drippings, the garlic, the mustard, and the vinegar. Taste and correct the seasoning with salt and pepper. Heat half the dressing and toss the cabbage in the pan with the dressing to warm it through. Transfer the cabbage to a serving platter or individual plates.

Crumble the goat cheese and the bacon over the cabbage. Spoon the remaining dressing over the top and sprinkle with the pecans. Serve immediately.

Warm Leek, Potato & Artichoke Salad
with Mustard Vinaigrette

Serves 6 to 8 as a side dish

This is a lovely salad for spring, when artichokes are in season and at their best. You can prepare the potatoes, artichokes, leeks, and eggs several hours or even a day before serving this irresistibly delicious salad. Remove all the ingredients from the refrigerator an hour before serving and then warm each item, separately, in a sauté pan before assembling the salad.

Mustard Vinaigrette, page 226, made with Green Peppercorn mustard
1½ pounds small new potatoes, preferably creamers, scrubbed
Kosher salt
4 large pastured eggs
8 small or 4 large leeks, washed thoroughly, all green parts trimmed away
3 tablespoons olive oil
4 large artichokes, trimmed and boiled until just tender
2 tablespoons snipped chives
2 tablespoons minced fresh Italian parsley
Black pepper in a mill
4 cups mustard sprouts, page 275, or pea shoots

Make the vinaigrette and set it aside.

Put the potatoes into a medium saucepan, cover by 2 inches with water, and add a generous 2 tablespoons of salt. Bring to a boil over high heat, reduce the heat, and simmer gently until the potatoes are tender but not falling apart. To test for doneness, press a bamboo skewer through a potato; there should be just a tad of resistance. Drain the potatoes, put them in a wide shallow serving bowl, and cover with a tea towel to keep warm.

While the potatoes cook, put the eggs into a small saucepan, cover with water, and bring to a boil over medium heat. Simmer gently for 5 minutes, cover the pan, remove from the heat, and let sit undisturbed for 15 minutes. Drain, transfer to an ice water bath, and cool for 15 minutes. Crack the shells all over and return to the ice water for 15 minutes more. Peel the eggs carefully, and pat them dry with a clean tea towel. Cut the eggs into lengthwise quarters.

Cut the leeks into 1-inch diagonal slices; check for sand and dirt and rinse in warm water if necessary. Put the leeks in a sauté pan, cover with water, and set over high heat. When the water boils, reduce the heat and simmer very gently for 5 minutes. Drain, add the olive oil, and reduce to the heat. Sauté for 3 to 4 minutes, until the leeks are tender but not completely soft. Season with salt and set aside.

Remove the artichoke leaves from the hearts, set the leaves aside for another use, and, using a sharp paring knife, cut out the chokes. Trim the hearts and cut each one into 6 wedges.

To assemble the salad, spread the mustard sprouts or pea shoots over a serving platter or individual plates.

Cut the potatoes into pieces about the same size as the artichoke hearts and put them into a medium bowl; add the leeks and artichoke hearts and toss the vegetables together gently. Add half the dressing, chives, and parsley, toss gently, taste, and correct for salt. Spoon the vegetables on the platter or plates. Scatter quartered eggs on top, add the remaining dressing, season with salt and pepper, and serve right away.

Variation:
- For a heartier salad, steam 3 pounds PEI mussels in a little white wine and lemon juice until they pop open, about five minutes. Cool, remove the mussels from their shells, and toss with about 3 tablespoons of the dressing. Add to the salad just before adding the eggs.

Sandwiches, Tarts & Strudels

"In my courtroom, putting mayo on a corned beef sandwich is a felony. Twenty years!"

This line is from a cartoon by Dennis Schmidt that is included in the book *Habeas Codfish: Reflections On Food and the Law* by Barry M. Levenson, founder of Mount Horeb Mustard Museum.

At Katz's Deli in New York City, customers are warned to ask for mayo on their pastrami sandwiches "at their own peril." An earlier version of a menu warns "don't even think about asking for mayonnaise!"

The Order of the Bath, a short silent film made in about 1922 by Benson's, an advertising agency in London, under the guise of "The Mustard Club" shows a sandwich giving evidence in a courtroom about a man who indulged in a buffet without mustard. The accused has come down with a cold and his omission of mustard is said to be the cause. The offender is sentenced to a mustard bath, using Colman's Bath Mustard. Colman's, of course, was the client and Dorothy L. Sayers, author of the Peter Wimsey mystery series, the account executive. The film is included in Mustard: The Spice of Nations, one of a number of films under the Spice of Life umbrella. It can be found on youtube.com

These lighthearted warnings reflect long-held sentiments about what we spread on our sandwiches. And although I do love mayonnaise and could even go so far as to describe a BLT without mayo as a crime, the dishes here, from the humble hotdog to a posh leek strudel, require mustard.

It's the law!

Or should be.

Hot Dog
Carrot Dog
Summer Tomato Sandwich
Grilled Chicken Sandwich with Mustard Sprouts and Mustard
Vinaigrette
Chicken Sandwich on Walnut Bread with Honey Mustard
Bockwurst Sandwiches with Onion-Mustard Sauce
Lamb Burgers with Mustard Butter
French Lamb Loaf
Ploughman's Lunch
Shooter's Sandwich
Leek & Mustard Tart
Leek Strudel

Hot Dog

Serves 6

Do we need an actual recipe for hot dogs? Not really but because of its importance to American mustard, I must include it here. There are many regional and national variations, of course, from simple hot dogs with ketchup, which seem to be a favorite with toddlers everywhere, and corn dogs doused with mustard to chili dogs, chili cheese dogs, Kansas City's Reuben hot dogs, Chicago-style hot dogs with hot peppers, onions, tomatoes, pickles, and green relish, Milwaukee hot dogs served on hard rolls, and Hawaiian Puka Dogs, with Polish sausage on Hawaiian sweet bread topped with tropical fruit salsa. There are BLT hot dogs, hot dogs buried in a pile of cole slaw, hot dogs wrapped in bacon, and so many other variations. We're a country obsessed.

Sometimes a hot dog hits the spot like nothing else and when I find I'm jonesin' for one, this is typically how I like it, though it is rare to find a whole wheat bun, other than in my own kitchen.

6 beef hot dogs, such as Niman Fearless Franks
6 whole wheat hot dog buns
1 cup sauerkraut, preferably homemade
½ small red onion, cut into small dice
Mustard of choice

Put the hot dogs on a hot grill, in a toaster oven set on broil, or in a hot oven and cut, turning a few times, until they just begin to crack open and are sizzling hot.

While the hot dogs cook, toast the buns to whatever degree of doneness you prefer.

Set the toasted buns on a clean work surface, open them, and put sauerkraut down the center of each. Set the hot dogs on top, scatter onion over them, and squirt or slather plenty of mustard over everything.

Enjoy right away.

Carrot Dog

Serves 2, easily increased

    I am not a fan of faux meat, of soy or wheat protein seasoned to resemble the flavor of whatever meat one is trying to imitate. I find both the flavors and textures unpleasant and insipid, so no soy dogs for me, thank you! I was thrilled when my local Grange Hall in Sebastopol served carrot hot dogs as a vegetarian option at a fall event a couple of years ago. What a brilliant idea! Here's my version.

2 whole medium carrots, scrubbed or peeled and trimmed
Olive oil
2 whole wheat hot dog buns
¼ cup sauerkraut
2 tablespoons minced red onion
Mustard of choice

Roast or steam the carrots whole until quite tender; the exact time will vary depending on the exact size of the carrot.

When the carrots are tender, quickly toast the buns, set them on a work surface, and divide the sauerkraut between them. Top with a carrot, add onions, and squirt or slather mustard on top.

Enjoy right away .

Summer Tomato Sandwich

Serves 1, easily increased

A tomato sandwich is one of the simplest joys of summer. This one combines mustard vinaigrette with other vegetables, perfect when you have some leftover potatoes on hand. Change it up as you like—add thin slices of cucumber or zucchini, roasted peppers, or sliced hard-boiled eggs—sit back, and enjoy the season.

2 slices of sturdy hearth bread, preferably sourdough, lightly toasted
3 tablespoons Mustard Vinaigrette, page 226
2 very small cooked potatoes, very thinly sliced
Kosher salt
1 thin slice of red onion
1 ripe backyard-quality tomato, cut into ¼-inch rounds, ends discarded
Black pepper in a mill
2 radishes, very thinly sliced
Handful of Mustard Sprouts, page 275, or shredded cabbage

Set the toasted bread on a clean work surface and brush both pieces with some of the vinaigrette.

Spread the potatoes on the bottom piece, season with salt, and arrange the onion on top. Add the sliced tomatoes, overlapping them slightly, and season with salt and several turns of black pepper.

Top with radishes and either the sprouts or cabbage. Drizzle the remaining dressing over the sandwich, add the top piece of bread, and enjoy right away or wrap in wax paper and aluminum foil and enjoy within a few hours.

Grilled Chicken Sandwich
with Mustard Sprouts and Mustard Vinaigrette

Serves 2, easily increased

For the most part, I've always felt less is more when it comes to salads, sandwiches, and many other dishes. If I'm getting a sandwich at a deli, for example, I don't automatically choose the default combination of onion, lettuce, tomato, mustard, and mayonnaise. Instead, I select the additions that I think will most flatter the main ingredient. In this sandwich, I find lettuce and tomato interfere with other flavors and textures and so I don't recommend adding them. If you don't want to bother with the sprouts, simply leave them off; the sandwich will still be delicious.

2 plump chicken thighs or 1 full breast, cut in half, de-boned
Kosher salt
Black pepper in a mill
2 French rolls, split
Dijon mustard
4 thin slices of sweet onion
Mustard Vinaigrette, page 226
Handful of Mustard Sprouts, page 275, other sprouts, or pea shoots

Put the chicken, one piece at a time, between 2 sheets of wax paper and pound it with a meat tenderizer, turning once, until it flattens a bit. Season the chicken all over with salt and pepper and grill it over hot coals or on a stove top grill or grill pan until it is just done, about 5 minutes per side. *Do not overcook it.* Transfer to a small plate, cover with a lid or sheet of aluminum foil, and set aside briefly.

Toast the rolls and set them, opened, on a clean work surface. Slather mustard on the cut surfaces and set the onions on top. Add the chicken, spoon vinaigrette on top, add sprouts, and put the top piece of bread in place.

Cut the sandwiches in half and serve right away.

Chicken Sandwich on Walnut Bread
with Honey Mustard

Serves 2, easily increased

I have noticed that amateur cooks, inexperienced cooks, and even young chefs rub condiments into the bread when making a sandwich. This is simply a bad technique that results in an inferior tasting sandwich, no matter the quality of the ingredients. Condiments, no matter what they are, should be slathered on in a single, light stroke. The best way to accomplish this is with a flexible medium-sized rubber spatula. And remember, a single stroke across the bread, not pressing down into the bread, is all that is needed.

4 thick slices walnut bread, toasted
Honey-Pepper Mustard, page 241, or commercial honey mustard
Leftover roasted chicken
Kosher salt
Black pepper in a mill
Handful of greens, such as frisee, arugula, or shredded cabbage

Set the toasted bread on a clean work surface, slather mustard generously over each slice, and mound chicken on two pieces. Season with salt and pepper, top with the greens, add the second piece of bread, and enjoy right away.

Bockwurst Sandwiches
with Onion-Mustard Sauce

Serves 4

Simple, easy to make, and full of great flavor, this classic German-inspired pub sandwich is irresistible. I had my first taste of it when I was in Zurich for a few days, following a lengthy visit to India. Exhausted from the flight, I went to bed early in a hotel that sat above a pub. The aromas of the grilled bockwurst enticed me out of bed, into my clothes, and downstairs, where I enjoyed the sandwich and a glass of beer. I returned to bed, thinking I would finally sleep. This scene played out not once, not twice, but three times, until I was finally sated and calm enough to sleep.

American bockwurst are closer to what the German's call weisswurst, a white sausage made of veal and pork which has its roots in Bavaria, where they are typically poached. I prefer them grilled or cooked under a hot broiler. If you have a toaster oven, it will work perfectly with these sausages.

2 tablespoons olive oil	Black pepper in a mill
1 pound yellow onions, thinly sliced	4 bockwurst
Kosher salt	4 tablespoons coarse-grain mustard
1 cup beef stock	4 sourdough French rolls, split

Prepare a charcoal fire or preheat an oven broiler.

Set a heavy frying pan over medium heat, add the olive and onion, and sauté until very soft and fragrant, about 15 minutes. Season with salt, add the stock, and simmer for 5 minutes. Season with several turns of black pepper, stir in the mustard, and remove from the heat. Taste and correct the seasoning as necessary. Set aside.

Grill or broil the sausages for about 15 minutes, turning to brown all sides, or until they burst open.

While the sausage cooks, toast the French rolls.

Place a sausage in each roll and spoon the onion mixture on top.

Enjoy right away.

Beverage Recommendation: Best with chilled hard cider or beer.

Lamb Burgers
with Mustard Butter

Serves 4

To make the very best (and safest) burgers, grind the meat yourself or ask your butcher to do it for you. Grass-fed and pastured meats require different cooking than standard commercial meats. They need higher heat and shorter time to cook, so adjust according to the type of meat your are using and your personal preferences. I like my burgers, no matter the kind of meat, rare, and have since I was a small child. These days we are advised to never eat rare meat but it is a risk I am comfortable taking, as I pay attention to the source of the meat I buy and I employ sensible sanitary practices in my kitchen.

1¼ pound freshly ground grass-fed lamb
Kosher salt
Black pepper in a mill
4 rounds, ¼-inch thick, of Mustard Butter, chilled, page 220
4 rolls of choice, such as ciabatta, French roll, etc.
Dijon mustard
Best-quality mayonnaise, optional
4 thin slices of red onion
Dill pickles

Put the lamb into a mixing bowl, season with salt and pepper, and mix gently. Transfer to a clean work surface, divide into four equal portions, and shape each piece into ball.

Hold one ball in your non-dominant hand and, with your other hand, press a round of butter into the center, closing the meat all around it. Set the ball on the work surface and gently pat it until it forms a patty ¾-inch thick. Set all of the formed patties on a platter and chill for 30 minutes.

Preheat a stove-top grill or cast iron frying pan over high heat. When quite hot, add the lamb burgers and cook for 2 minutes. Turn and cook for 3 minutes more or a tad longer for medium rare to rare.

A Mustard Cookbook

Toast the rolls while the burgers cook. Set them on a clean work surface, spread mustard over each piece or spread mustard on the bottom pieces and mayonnaise on the top.

Transfer the burgers to the rolls, setting them on the bottom piece. Top with red onion, add the top piece of bread, and enjoy immediately, with dill pickles alongside.

> **Variation:**
> - Make the burgers using freshly ground beef, bison, goat, or duck.

French Lamb Loaf

Serves 6

Removing the insides of a loaf of sourdough bread creates a wonderful container to hold all manner of meat and vegetable mixtures. In this one, I combine a suave French mustard with lamb and French feta cheese. The loaf makes a great picnic item but it should be wrapped—several layers of newspaper work well—and kept hot during transport. And don't forget to take along plenty of additional Dijon mustard.

1 long loaf of San Francisco-style sourdough bread
Olive oil
1 small yellow onion, diced
Kosher salt
1 pound freshly ground lamb
2 tablespoons minced garlic
1 pastured egg, beaten
3 tablespoons + 2 teaspoons Dijon mustard

2 tablespoons finely minced fresh Italian parsley
1 teaspoon finely minced fresh rosemary
Black pepper in a mill
4 ounces French feta, broken into chunks
2 tablespoons butter

Preheat the oven to 375 degrees.

Cut the ends off the loaf of bread and, with your fingers, pull out the soft insides of the bread, making a shell. Set the ends aside.

Set a frying pan over medium heat, add a bit of olive oil, and add the bread you have pulled out. Turning it frequently, cook until it is dry and crumbly. Transfer to a bowl, cool, and crush into crumbs.

Return the pan to the heat, add a little more oil, and sauté the onion until soft and fragrant. Season with salt. Add the lamb and cook, breaking it up with a fork, until it loses its raw color. Add the garlic, sauté 2 minutes more, add the breadcrumbs, and remove from the heat.

Mix together the egg, 3 tablespoons of the mustard, the parsley, and the rosemary and stir into the meat once it has cooled a bit. Season with salt and pepper and cool until easy to handle. Add the feta and use two forks to toss gently.

Use your hands or a large spoon, press the meat mixture into the hollowed out bread, packing it fairly tightly. Set the loaf on a large sheet of aluminum foil and add the ends to close the loaf.

Put the butter in a small saucepan, add the remaining mustard and brush it all over the outside of the loaf. Wrap tightly in the aluminum foil, set on the middle rack of the oven, and cook for 20 minutes, until the loaf is lightly toasted on the outside and sizzling hot inside.

Let the loaf rest for 5 minutes before cutting it into 1½-inch thick slices; serve right away, with plenty of Dijon alongside.

Ploughman's Lunch

Serves 3 or 4

Today, we see Ploughman's Lunch offered in British-style taverns throughout the United States, but its history extends back to England, where it was the traditional midday meal, packed in a lunch tin and eaten in the fields. At its core is good bread, English cheese, mustard, chutney, and beer, with pickles, fruit, hard-boiled eggs, and some sort of meat as common additions. Variations on this theme are nearly endless and even somewhat arbitrary. Use what appeals to you and what you may have on hand.

4 deviled eggs, page 121
1 apple or other seasonal fruit
Pickles or cornichons
8 ounces salami, dry sausage or
    similar cured meat
1 wedge of cheese, 4 to 6 ounces,
    such as Huntsman (pictured),
    Montgomery Cheddar, or
    Cotswold

2 tablespoons Onion Chutney, page 265,
    or other chutney of choice, in a
    small bowl
2 tablespoons coarse-grain mustard,
    in a small bowl
1 rustic baguette
Chilled hard cider, pilsner, or other
    beverage of choice

Make the deviled eggs, if you have not already done so.

Set all the ingredients on some sort of flat serving platter, preferably made of wood. Add appropriate implements, set the bread alongside, and enjoy, using your hands to tear off pieces of bread.

Shooter's Sandwich

Serves 6 to 8

While the ploughmen were enjoying their rustic lunches out in the fields, hunters were tucking into this remarkably delicious sandwich.

1 round loaf of rustic hearth bread
3 tablespoons butter
2 shallots, minced
1 pound specialty mushrooms, such as maitake, chanterelle, or oyster, broken into pieces
¾ cup dry white wine
Kosher salt
Black pepper in a mill
3 tablespoons chopped fresh Italian parsley

2 boned grass-fed ribeye steaks, about 1 pound each
Coarse-grain mustard
½ cup dry red wine
Dijon mustard
Dill pickles
Quince Mostarda, page 263, or Onion Chutney, page 265

Cut off the top of the bread just before the loaf begins to flare out. Use your fingers to pull out as much of the bread as possible from the main part of the loaf; reserve the bread to make breadcrumbs for another use.

Set the bread aside.

Put the butter into a large sauté pan set over medium-low heat, add the shallots, and sauté until soft and fragrant, about 7 to 8 minutes. Add the mushrooms, turn to coat them in butter, add the wine, cover the pan, and cook until the mushrooms are limp; time will vary depending on the type of mushrooms. When the mushrooms have wilted, remove the lid and continue to cook until all the liquid is reduced and the mushrooms are very tender. Season with salt and several very generous turns of black pepper. Stir in the parsley and remove from the heat.

Set a cast iron frying pan over high heat. Season the steaks all over with salt and pepper, pressing the pepper into the meat. Gently brush the steaks with coarse-grain mustard. When the pan is very hot, add the steaks and cook for 3 minutes. Turn and cook 3 minutes more or just a bit longer for medium rare. (If using corn-fed beef, cook about 4 to 5 minutes per side.)

Carefully add the red wine, standing back as it will likely flare up. When the wine is completely reduced, transfer the steaks to a plate.

Spread Dijon mustard over the inside of the bread shell and press a steak into it. Spoon the mushrooms on top and spread them evenly. Top with the second steak. Spread Dijon over the inside of the bread's crown and set it on top. Wrap the sandwich in a large sheet of parchment and tie it in place with kitchen twine.

Set the sandwich between two heavy cutting boards and set weights (large cans of tomatoes or a couple of bricks, for example) on the top board. Set in a cool place for at least 4 hours and as long as overnight.

To enjoy, cut the sandwich in wide slices or wedges and serve with pickles and mostarda or chutney.

Beverage suggestions: This robust sandwich cries out for a bold beverage that will stand up to it, such as your favorite beer or ale or a rustic red wine.

Leek & Mustard Tart

Serves 6

Leeks and mustard enjoy a delicious camaraderie, expressed here in a delicate tart. I love leeks, and this creamy tart is rich with their flavor, which blends wonderfully with the mustard. Serve this tart as the main course of a light lunch, brunch, or summer dinner, accompanied by a delicate chilled soup, perhaps, and a salad with lots of crunch in it.

3 tablespoons butter
5 cups sliced (¼-inch thick) leeks,
    with 2 inches of green stems
½ cup dry white wine
Kosher salt
Black pepper in a mill
3 eggs

1½ cups heavy cream
¼ cup Dijon mustard, plus more for
    the tart shell
4 ounces chèvre
2 tablespoons snipped fresh chives
1 partially baked 10-inch tart shell

Preheat the oven to 350 degrees.

Melt the butter in a heavy skillet. Add the leeks and sauté for 5 minutes. Add the wine and simmer until it evaporates. Season to taste with salt and pepper and remove from the heat.

Mix together the eggs, heavy cream, the ¼ cup mustard, and the chevre. Brush the surface of the tart shell with mustard and spread the leeks evenly on top. Pour in the custard, agitate the pan gently, and sprinkle with chives.

Variation:
- Omit the butter. Sauté 4 slices of bacon until just crisp, drain on absorbent paper, and sauté the leeks in the bacon drippings. Chop or crumble the bacon over the tart before adding the chives.

Leek Strudel

Serves 8

If you are nervous about making dough, this is a great place to start, as it is nearly foolproof and does not require any special skill. The results are absolutely delicious.

For the dough:
1 cup (2 sticks) unsalted butter, at room temperature
8 ounces old-fashioned style cream cheese
2½ cups unbleached flour
2 teaspoons kosher salt
¼ cup heavy cream

For the filling:
2 tablespoons olive oil
2 pounds leeks, white and 2 inches of green, thoroughly washed, trimmed, and sliced
2 sweet onions, thinly sliced
5 cloves garlic, minced
Kosher salt
Black pepper in a mill
Salt and freshly ground black pepper
3 tablespoons Dijon mustard, plus more for serving
4 ounces Gruyere, Joe Matos St. George, or similar cheese, grated
2 tablespoons snipped fresh chives
1 egg white, lightly beaten with 1 tablespoon of water

First, make the dough. Put the butter and cream cheese into the work bowl of an electric mixer and mix on medium until smooth. Slowly add the flour and the salt, mixing all the while. Add the cream, mix well, and turn out onto a clean work surface. Press the dough into a ball, wrap it tightly, and chill it thoroughly. The dough can be made up to 2 days in advance.

To make the filling, heat the butter in a heavy skillet. Sauté the leeks and onions until limp. Add the garlic and sauté for another 2 minutes. Season with salt and pepper, stir in a tablespoon of the mustard, and set aside to cool.

Preheat the oven to 400 degrees.

Sprinkle a clean work surface with flour and roll out the chilled dough into a rectangle measuring 10-inches-by-12-inches. Brush the surface of the dough with the mustard.

Spoon the leek filling down the center of the dough and sprinkle the cheese on top, followed by the chives.

Fold the pastry over to form a long cylinder and seal the edges with egg wash; use the tines of a fork to press the edges of the dough together. Brush the top of the pastry with egg wash and sprinkle with salt. Using a sharp knife, make crosswise slashes through the top layer of the pastry at 2-inch intervals. Carefully transfer the strudel to a baking sheet.

Set the baking sheet on the middle rack of the oven and bake until golden brown, about 20 to 25 minutes. Remove from the oven, let rest 10 minutes, cut into slices, and serve warm, with Dijon alongside.

Eggs

"To make an omelette," Joan Didion writes in "The Women's Movement," a chapter in *The White Album*, her second collection of essays, " you need not only those broken eggs but some 'oppressed' to break them . . ."

It's rare that I take an egg in hand without thinking of this passage, which opens Didion's characteristically piercing exploration of the Women's Moment as it was in the 1970s.

It's not that I feel oppressed as I make an omelette or crack an egg for any other reason. It's that I love Didion's prose and always smile at her observations, including this one, and the way in which an egg—and by extension, cooking—is often used a symbol of oppression, especially in regards to women.

There is often an element of oppression in an egg but I don't believe it is of the person doing the cooking. Rather, it is in the millions of commercial hens, forced to live in tiny cages stacked one on top of the other in twenty-four-hour light to speed up their laying cycle. It is a miserable and cruel life.

Raising chickens is now a popular pursuit throughout much of America and it is easy to find pastured eggs almost anywhere but especially at farmers' markets. I encourage you to find a source if you have not already done so. At first, you may cringe at the difference in price but you will, before long, find it worth it, not only because it's the right thing to do and the eggs taste better, but also because you'll be more satisfied with them, which in turn may lead to buying fewer eggs. When something gives us full satisfaction, we are much more easily sated.

Perfect Deviled Eggs
Deviled Egg Salad
Scrambled Eggs & Mustard Greens with The Devil's Mustard
Spring Omelet with Mustard
Souffléd Omelet with Mustard Butter & Dijon Pear Sauce
Mustard Frittata with Potatoes & Asparagus
Gruyère Soufflé with Dijon Pear Sauce

Perfect Deviled Eggs

Serves 4 to 6

It's important to know how to make perfect deviled eggs, a classic American appetizer and picnic dish. A purist, I eschew additions such as pickle relish, capers, minced onions, or olives. I think making deviled eggs with Miracle Whip is a travesty. But I believe that good mustard is absolutely essential. Made only with mayonnaise, there's no devil; it's the mustard that provides the kick that warrants the name. Deviled ham, deviled crab, and other foods with the moniker typically refer to both mustard and, frequently, ground chilies or other spicy additions.

6 large fresh eggs
⅓ to ½ cup mayonnaise
3 tablespoons Dijon mustard
Dash of Tabasco Sauce
2 teaspoons black peppercorns, crushed
¾ teaspoon kosher salt

Put the eggs in a in a medium saucepan and cover with water by at least 1 inch. Set over medium heat, bring to a boil, simmer gently for 3 to 4 minutes, cover, remove from the heat, and let rest for 15 minutes. Transfer the eggs to a cold-water bath, changing the water two or three times as it warms. Add ice to the water, crack each egg all over, and let it rest in the ice water for another 15 minutes. Carefully peel the cooled eggs, rinse off any bits of shell, dry them on a tea towel, and cut them in half lengthwise. Scoop out the yolks and leave the whites on your work surface.

Press the yolks through a potato ricer into a bowl or place them in the bowl and mash them with a fork. Mix in ⅓ cup of the mayonnaise, the mustard, Tabasco, pepper, and salt. If the mixture seems a little dry, add the remaining mayonnaise. Taste and correct for salt. Fill the centers of the egg whites with the egg yolk mixture, cover with plastic wrap, and refrigerate for at least 30 minutes before serving.

Deviled Egg Salad

Serves 4 to 6

This recipe is a great alternative to deviled eggs, especially when you have such fresh eggs that they are nearly impossible to peel without tearing them apart. When this happens, simple break the eggs in half, use a spoon to scoop them out of their shells, put them in a bowl and use a large fork or a pastry cutter to break them into small, somewhat even pieces.

¼ cup, approximately, Mustard Vinaigrette, page 226

6 pastured eggs

4 tablespoons homemade or Best Foods/Hellmans brand mayonnaise

1 tablespoon Dijon mustard, plus more to taste

Kosher salt

Black pepper in a mill

4 to 6 cups fresh salad greens

Make the vinaigrette if you do not already have it on hand.

To cook the eggs, put them in a saucepan, cover with water by at least 1 inch, and set over medium-high heat. When the water boils, simmer very gently for 5 minutes, cover, and remove from the heat. Let rest for 15 minutes. Transfer the eggs to an ice water bath, lightly cracking the shells all over on a hard surface, and let them rest for at least 15 minutes.

Carefully peel the eggs so that they remain intact as much as possible.

Dry the eggs on a tea towel.

Using an egg slicer, cut each egg three times, carefully turning it each time, so that you end up with small cubes.

Put the eggs into a mixing bowl, add the mayonnaise and mustard, and mix well. Season with salt and pepper, taste, and correct for salt and mustard.

Put the salad greens into a large bowl, season with a little salt, and toss. Add a tablespoon of vinaigrette and toss again.

Divide the greens among individual salad plates or bowls and top with egg salad. Add a dollop of vinaigrette to each portion and serve right away.

A Mustard Cookbook

Scrambled Eggs & Mustard Greens
with The Devil's Mustard

Serves 4

The Devil's Mustard, page 239
3 tablespoons Mustard Butter, page 220
½ bunch (about 3 to 4 large leaves) mustard greens, trimmed and chopped
6 to 8 pastured eggs, well beaten
Kosher salt
Black pepper in a mill
4 thick slices of hearth bread, lightly toasted

Make the mustard and set it aside.

Melt 2 tablespoons of the Mustard Butter in a heavy sauté pan set over medium heat, add the mustard greens and a splash of water, cover, and cook until wilted and tender, about 7 to 8 minutes. Season with salt and pepper and tip into a small bowl; cover and keep warm.

Increase the heat to high and add the remaining tablespoon of butter. While the butter melts, add two tablespoons of water to the eggs, season generously with salt and pepper, and mix well.

When the butter is very hot and foamy, tip in the eggs and let cook without stirring for 90 seconds. Break up with a fork, turning the eggs so that they cook evenly. Pull them off the heat the moment they lose their raw look but be certain not to let them become dry.

Working quickly, set a piece of toast on individual plates. Fold the wilted greens into the eggs and spoon on top of the toast. Add a dollop of mustard and serve right away, with the remaining mustard alongside.

Spring Omelet
with Mustard

Serves 1

When you rely on eggs from local hens, either from your own flock, a neighbor's flock, or a local farmer's flock, there is something very special about spring eggs, a delicacy, a tenderness, a subtle thrill. The hens have triumphed over winter and are enjoying the light and warmth. Commercially produced eggs offer none of this and there is a uniform blandness to the eggs of these miserable hens. I have heard certain nationally-known writers say that paying more to eat eggs from pastured hens is an act of faith and compassion only because the eggs taste no different. Those who say this either have very dull palates or have actually never taken the leap. There is no comparison and once you understand it, it is impossible to be satisfied with factory-farm eggs.

If you will be feeding more than one person, it is best to simply make individual omelets and not a bigger omelet to share.

1 teaspoon Dijon mustard
2 large pastured eggs, beaten until smooth
Kosher salt
Black pepper in a mill
2 teaspoons butter, preferably from grass-fed cows
1 garlic clove, preferably fresh (not cured), cut in half
2 ounces grated Montgomery Cheddar or other artisan Cheddar
Dollop of Quince Mostarda, page 263
Toasted and buttered hearth bread

Add the mustard to the eggs, season with salt and pepper, and mix well.

Set an omelet pan over high heat, add the butter, and, when it is melted, add the garlic. Cook for about 15 seconds, spear the garlic with a fork, and rub it all over the pan; discard it.

Pour the eggs into the pan and let cook for 90 seconds. Use a fork to stir the uncooked portion of the eggs, being certain not to disturb the cooked layer, until they are cooked as you like them.

Scatter the cheese down the center of the omelet.

Use your non-dominant hand to hold the handle of the pan, with your fingers on top. Tip the pan slightly and use a fork or rubber spatula to fold about a third of the omelet over itself. Increase the angle, holding the pan over a plate, and let the omelet roll out as it folds one more time, which is to say in thirds.

Add a spoonful of mostarda alongside and enjoy immediately.

Serving Suggestions: with roasted spring onions; with roasted asparagus; with sliced and sautéed radishes.

Souffléd Omelet
with Mustard Butter and Dijon Pear Sauce

Serves 3 to 4

A souffléd omelette, sometimes called a puffed or puffy omelet, takes a bit more time to make than other types of omelets, but it isn't difficult and has a lovely ethereal quality, like a spring cloud. It makes a lovely dinner when you serve a big green salad alongside and is, of course, a lovely breakfast on a weekend morning when you can linger.

Dijon Pear Sauce, page 233
3 tablespoons Mustard Butter, chilled
6 large pastured eggs, separated into large bowls
Kosher salt
Black pepper in a mill
¼ cup cold water

Make the Dijon Pear Sauce and set it aside.

Preheat the oven to 350 degrees.

Cut 1 tablespoon of the Mustard Butter into small pieces and add it to the egg yolks, along with a few pinches of kosher salt and several turns of black pepper. Whisk thoroughly and set aside.

Whisk or beat the egg whites until they are quite foamy. Add the cold water and continue to whisk until the eggs form soft peaks that hold their shape when the mixer or whisk is lifted. Use a flexible rubber spatula to gently fold the yolks into the whites, being sure not to over-mix, as you don't want to lose the egg whites' loft.

Put the remaining 2 tablespoons of butter into a heavy pan, preferably one with sloping sides, such as an All Clad Saucier. Alternately, use a cast iron frying pan. Set over medium heat and when the butter is melted, tip the pan to coat the sides with the butter.

Pour the egg mixture into the pan and, without stirring, cook for 3 to 4 minutes, until the bottom and sides are set. Transfer to the oven and cook until the omelet is puffed, the middle set, and the top lightly browned, about 12 minutes or a bit longer.

Remove from the oven and use a rubber spatula to loosen the sides. Cut the omelet into wedges, set on individual plates, and top with some of the sauce. Serve right away.

Variation:
- While the omelet is in the oven, cook 3 big handfuls of baby spinach in a little butter until it is just wilted. Add 2 or 3 pressed garlic cloves, season with salt and pepper, and remove from the heat. When the omelet is done, put the spinach on one side of it, fold the omelet over, tip onto a plate, top with sauce, and serve.

- While the omelet cooks in the oven, cut a firm-ripe pear in half, remove its core, and cut into lengthwise slices. Sauté in butter until just tender and season with a pinch of salt and several generous turns of black pepper. When the omelet is done, put the pears on one side of it, fold the omelet over, tip onto a plate, top with sauce, and serve.

Mustard Frittata
with Potatoes & Asparagus

Serves 4

A properly made frittata is more than just an open-faced omelet, as it is sometimes called. A frittata has a creamier texture and is really another thing altogether. It is an excellent main course for breakfast, brunch, or lunch, and can be varied to incorporate whatever seasonal vegetables or herbs you have. This version is my favorite, especially when I make it with tiny Yellow Finn potatoes from my garden.

1 pound asparagus, tough stems snapped off, roasted until tender (see note below)
½ cup extra virgin olive oil
Kosher salt
Black pepper in a mill
4 small, waxy potatoes (Yellow Finn, Rose Fir, or new red), unpeeled, boiled until just tender
6 eggs
3 tablespoons plus 1 teaspoon Dijon mustard, plus additional mustard for serving
2 teaspoons butter
1 teaspoon brown sugar
3 tablespoons balsamic vinegar, plus vinegar for brushing on top

Slice the potatoes into very thin rounds. Break the eggs into a large mixing bowl, add the 3 tablespoons mustard, and whisk together vigorously. Season the eggs with the 1 teaspoon salt and several turns of black pepper.

Melt the butter in a 10-inch cast iron skillet over high heat. Make sure the butter coats the entire pan. Spread the potatoes over the surface, pour the eggs in, and leave over the heat for 1 minute. Transfer the pan to a 275°F oven and bake until the eggs are set, about 12 to 14 minutes. Be sure not to overcook.

Whisk together the remaining teaspoon mustard, the brown sugar, the 3 tablespoons balsamic vinegar, and the olive oil. Season to taste with salt and pepper.

Remove the pan from the oven, brush the surface of the frittata with a thin film of balsamic vinegar, and top it with a few more turns of black pepper. Let the frittata rest for 5 minutes and then remove it from the pan, loosening it with a knife if it sticks. Arrange the asparagus spears on a large platter or on 4 individual plates and drizzle with a bit of the vinaigrette. Carefully slice the frittata into strips about ⅛-inch wide and 3 inches long, and add them, randomly, to the plates or platter. Serve immediately, with additional mustard and the remaining vinaigrette on the side.

NOTE

To roast asparagus, preheat the oven to 450 degrees. Set the asparagus on a baking sheet, drizzle with a little olive oil, season with salt and pepper, and set on the middle rack of the oven. Cook until tender, about 5 to 6 minutes for thin stalks and as long as 12 minutes for fat one.

Variations:

- **Herb frittata:** Omit the potatoes. Add 2 tablespoons of chopped fresh herbs (oregano, marjoram, chives, thyme, summer savory) and ¾ cup freshly grated Romano cheese to the egg mixture and cook as directed.

- **Leek frittata:** Sauté the white part, sliced, of 2 leeks in butter, add it to the egg mixture, and cook as directed.

Gruyère Soufflé
with Dijon Pear Sauce

Serves 4 to 6 as a first course

A soufflé adds a special touch to a meal, a tenderness evoked by the delicate nature of the soufflé itself. But do not confuse a soufflé's delicacy with difficulty. Soufflés are really quite easy to make, and although they are beautiful when we first pull them from the oven, rising high as they do over the rim of the dish like a golden cloud, their almost immediate fall is not a sign of failure. Soufflés collapse on their own; it is their nature, as is their delicious taste.

1 cup heavy cream
1 cup half-and-half
5 ounces Gruyère cheese
4 egg yolks
3 to 4 tablespoons extra-forte Dijon
    mustard
Salt to taste, plus 1 teaspoon salt
Freshly ground black pepper

1 tablespoon butter
1½ teaspoons hot mustard flour
    (or Colman's dry mustard)
5 egg whites
Boiling water, as needed
Dijon Pear Sauce (page 233)
1 ripe pear

Place the cream and half-and-half in a heavy saucepan over medium heat and reduce by nearly half, being careful not to let the mixture boil over. Remove from the heat and let cool. Grate the Gruyère cheese and set it aside. Beat together the egg yolks and mustard and add them to the reduced cream. Add the grated cheese, stir to blend it in, and season to taste with salt and pepper. This part of the soufflé can be made in advance and set aside. Refrigerate if you will not use it within 30 minutes, but bring the mixture to room temperature before proceeding with the soufflé.

Preheat oven to 350°F. Butter a 1-quart soufflé dish. Stir together the 1 teaspoon salt and the mustard flour. Place the mixture in the soufflé dish and then shake the dish until it has coated the bottom and sides. Shake out any excess and set the soufflé dish aside.

A Mustard Cookbook

Beat the egg whites until stiff but not dry; gently and quickly fold them into the cream mixture. Using a rubber spatula to scrape the bowl, pour the soufflé mixture into the soufflé dish and place it in a large baking dish or pan. Pour boiling water to a depth of 2 inches into the baking dish.

Bake for 20 minutes; check carefully to see if it is done. The soufflé should have risen well above the dish and be a warm, toasty brown. Remove from the oven and serve immediately, with sliced pears and the Dijon Pear Sauce on the side.

Variation:
- Quickly sauté the pears in butter before serving them.

Flesh

If there is a type of meat that is not flattered by mustard, I have not yet found it. From a delicate filet of Petrale sole to a robust beef tenderloin or venison stew, the right mustard creates a perfect marriage, like the fictional Peter Wimsey and Harriet Vane, say, or the real-life Paul Newman and Joanne Woodward. It works so well that it can be hard to imagine one without the other. That was my goal as I wrote this chapter, to offer examples of the way mustard makes a dish soar, makes it more than the sum of its ingredients.

Where you source your ingredients is, of course, crucial. My guideline is to look for the closest sources so that I can avoid meats from factory farms, farmed fish, and commodity chicken. When you buy from small producers, you are supporting family farms, once the backbone of America, keeping more money in your community, supporting the best animal husbandry practices, and, almost as a bonus, securing the best tasting ingredients.

Deviled Crab Cakes
Braised Artichokes with Crab & Mustard Cream Dressing
Scallops in Lemon-Mustard Sauce with Favas & Fresh Fettuccini
Trout with Mushrooms & Mustard Breadcrumbs
Halibut Fillets with Olive Mustard & Breadcrumbs
Grilled Tuna with Black Bean, Pineapple & Serrano-Cilantro Mustard
Chicken Breasts Marinated in Mustard Oil with Radishes, Preserved
Lemons & Orzo
Chicken Legs Baked in Mustard
Chicken Dijonnaise
Chicken with Soft Polenta & Mustard Greens
Chicken Stew with Winter Squash & Mustard Greens
Seared Duck Breast with Cranberry-Mustard Sauce
Rabbit Dijonnaise

Rack of Lamb Dijonnaise
Oven-Roasted Leg of Lamb with Sausage Stuffing & Mustard Glaze
Lamb's Tongue in Saffron-Mustard Cream with Forbidden Rice
Poached Lamb & Goat Meat Loaf with Parsnip Puree
Southern-Style Mustard Greens & Ham Hocks with New Potatoes
Pork Loin with Apricot-Mustard Glaze
Slow-Roasted Pork Shoulder with Mustards & Herbs
Baby Back Ribs
Ham Steaks with Red-Eye Gravy & Grits
Country Ham with Red-Eye Gravy
Polenta with Sausages, Apples & Mustard Greens
Grilled Sausages & Onions with Assorted Mustards
Skirt Steak Dijon with Salsa Verde
Ribeye Steak with Red Wine Mustard Sauce
Beef Tongue in Mustard-Vinegar Sauce with Roasted Garlic &
Saffron-Mustard Cream
Beef Tongue with Mustard Cream, Radishes, & Watercress
Grilled Ribeye Steak with Fennel, Red Onions, Cucumbers &
Horseradish-Mustard Sauce
Honey-Mustard Steak with Basmati Rice
Beef Tenderloin with Mustard Butter & Roasted Shallot & Red Wine
Sauce

Deviled Crab Cakes

Makes about eight 3-inch cakes; serves 4

In The Chesapeake Bay Crab Cookbook (Aris Books/Addison-Wesley Publishing, 1991), Chef John Shields of Gertrude's Restaurant at the Baltimore Museum of Art offers several recipes combining mustard and crab, a culinary liaison of long and delicious duration. From soft-shell crabs slathered with Dijon, breaded, and panfried in butter, to a half-dozen variations on crab cakes, his recipes are spirited, easy to prepare, and simply really, really good. Similar to John's recipes, this version features mustard in both the crab cake itself and in the sauce that accompanies it. Unlike the traditional crab cakes of Chesapeake Bay, these cakes are bound with cream rather than mayonnaise. It is a wonderful version and has become a tradition in my home on New Year's Eve (and New Year's Day, too, if we have any left over). I use my local crab, the Dungeness, one of the great miracles of the Pacific.

3 tablespoons butter
¼ cup minced yellow onion
1 or 2 fresh serranos, minced
2/3 cup finely chopped celery
3 eggs, well beaten
¾ cup heavy cream, whipped until thick
2 tablespoons Dijon mustard, plus more to taste
2 tablespoons fresh lemon juice
1 tablespoon chopped fresh Italian parsley

About 3 cups fresh breadcrumbs or Mustard Breadcrumbs, page 262
3 cups freshly picked Dungeness crab meat, from about 2 medium crabs
Kosher salt
Black pepper in a mill
Serrano-Cilantro Mustard, page 245
Lime wedges
Chopped fresh cilantro

Melt 1 tablespoon of the butter in a sauté pan. Add the onion and sauté until transparent. Add the serranos and celery and sauté 5 minutes more. Remove from the heat and set aside to cool.

Add the vegetables to the beaten eggs and fold in the cream followed by the mustard, lemon juice, and parsley. Add 1 cup of the breadcrumbs, carefully fold in the crab, taste, and season with salt and pepper. Cover and chill for at least two hours and as long as overnight.

To make the cakes, heat the remaining 2 tablespoons of butter in a heavy skillet until foamy. If the crab mixture seems a little too moist, add another ½ cup to 1 cup of the remaining breadcrumbs and form cakes about 3 inches across.

Dust the cakes lightly with the breadcrumbs and sauté them, making sure not to crowd them in the skillet, for about 4 minutes. Turn and sauté 3 to 4 minutes more, until they are golden brown.

Set the crab cakes on individual plates, 2 per serving, and top each one with a bit of the mustard. Garnish with a wedge of lime and some cilantro and serve right away.

Beverage suggestions: dry sparkling wine, such as Iron Horse Vineyards Classic Brut.

Braised Artichokes
with Crab & Mustard Cream Dressing

Serves 4

When artichoke season arrives a bit early, in late winter, or when there's a late fall bumper crop, it coincides with the availability of fresh local Dungeness crab. This is my favorite way to serve them together. Use whatever crab is in season near you when artichokes are also available. If artichokes are hard to find, see the variation at the end of the recipe.

2 large artichokes, preferably Green Globe variety, trimmed and cut in half lengthwise
1 lemon
Kosher salt
Olive oil
½ cup crème fraîche
1 teaspoon prepared creamy horseradish
¼ cup Dijon mustard
1 tablespoon tomato paste
1 teaspoon sugar
1 teaspoons Tabasco sauce
Black pepper in a mill
Cooked crab meat of 1 medium or 2 small crabs, with leg meat set aside
1 tablespoon snipped fresh chives
2 hard-boiled eggs, cut in half lengthwise
2 tablespoons capers, drained

Use a small sharp knife to cut the choke from the artichoke hearts and squeeze a bit of lemon juice over the cut portions.

Put the artichokes into a saucepan that will hold them snugly in a single layer, season with salt, drizzle a bit of olive oil over them, and cover them with water. Set over medium heat and slowly bring to a boil. Reduce the heat and simmer gently until they are tender, about 15 to 20 minutes. Do not overcook; you want the hearts tender but not mushy.

Meanwhile, put the crème fraîche into a small bowl, add the horseradish, mustard, tomato paste, sugar, and Tabasco sauce and mix well. Add a generous squeeze of lemon juice, taste, correct for salt and acid, and season with several turns of black pepper. Cover and set aside.

Transfer the artichokes to a colander to drain thoroughly and set them on individual salad plates. Fill each artichoke with body meat and with about 2 tablespoons of the dressing. Set crab legs on top, add egg alongside, top it with a dollop of dressing, and scatter capers over everything.

Serve right away, with the remaining dressing alongside.

> **Variation:**
> - Instead of artichokes, use avocados. Cut two firm-ripe avocados in half lengthwise, use a soup spoon to carefully scoop out the flesh, and set a half avocado on each plate. Drizzle with a little lemon juice, season with salt and pepper, and continue as directed above.

Scallops in Lemon-Mustard Sauce
with Favas & Fresh Fettuccini

Serves 4

Fresh favas, once unheard of in the United States, are now popular at farmers' markets and grocery stores like Whole Foods for several weeks each spring. When they are not in season, you can make this dish without them or use English peas in their place.

⅔ to 1 cup shelled, blanched, and
    peeled favas
Kosher salt
10 ounces fresh (not dried) fettuccini
2 tablespoons all–purpose flour
1 teaspoon mustard flour (or
    Colman's dry mustard)
White pepper in a mill
1 pound bay or calico scallops, rinsed
    and patted dry with a tea towel

2 tablespoon butter
¼ cup white wine
Juice of ½ lemon
1 cup heavy cream
1 tablespoon Dijon mustard
Black pepper in a mill
1 tablespoon fresh snipped chives

Shell, blanch, and peel the favas if you have not already done so. Set them aside.

Fill a large pot two-thirds full with water, season generously with kosher salt, and bring to a boil over high heat. Add the fettuccini, stir until the water returns to a boil, and cook according to package instructions until just tender. Drain thoroughly and do not rinse.

While waiting for the water to boil, prepare the scallops. To do so, put the flour and mustard flour in a deep bowl or small paper bag and season generously with salt and several turns of white pepper. Add the scallops and stir or shake until they are evenly coated with the mixture. Transfer to a strainer and shake off the excess flour.

Put the butter into a medium sauté pan set over medium-high heat and when it is melted and foamy, add the scallops. Sauté quickly, tossing and shaking the pan to rotate the scallops and prevent them from burning. Cook until they are just done, about 3 minutes. Transfer to a bowl, cover with a tea towel, and keep warm.

Deglaze the pan with the white wine and lemon juice and simmer until only about 2 tablespoons remain. Lower the heat, add the cream, and simmer until it is reduced by one third. Remove the pan from the heat, stir in the Dijon, and season with several turns of black pepper. Taste and correct for salt.

Fold in the scallops and any juices that have collected in the bowl into the sauce, along with all but two tablespoons or so of the favas.

Divide the pasta among individual plates and top with the scallop mixture. Scatter the remaining favas and the chives on top and serve immediately.

Trout
with Mushrooms & Mustard Breadcrumbs

Serves 4

I love the delicate flavor and texture of trout, especially when I'm lucky enough to have some fresh-caught wild trout, right out of a river or lake. I usually prefer it prepared very simply, with a bit of butter, a squeeze of lemon, and a little salt. Every now and then, though, I like something a bit more elaborate and that's when I make this dish, which I serve with steamed rice, orzo, or couscous and steamed spinach.

4 rainbow trout, 8 to 10 ounces each
2 tablespoons butter
1 shallot, minced
3 cloves garlic, minced
Kosher salt
Black pepper in a mill
1 pound specialty mushrooms, such as maitake, oyster, or chanterelle, brushed clean and broken into small pieces

1 cup dry white wine
3 cups Mustard Breadcrumbs, page 262
3 tablespoons chopped fresh Italian parsley
2 tablespoons snipped fresh chives
1 lemon, halved
2 tablespoons Dijon mustard
2 tablespoons Mustard Butter, page 220
1 lemon, in wedges

Preheat the oven to 375 degrees.

Rinse the trout in cool water, pat them dry, and set them on a clean tea towel.

Put the butter into a heavy skillet set over medium-low heat, add the butter, and, when it is melted, sauté the shallots until soft and fragrant, about 7 minutes. Add the garlic and sauté 2 minutes more. Season with salt and pepper, increase the heat to high, add the mushrooms and the wine, cover and cook for 5 minutes. Uncover, lower the heat, and cook until the mushrooms are completely tender.

While the mushrooms cook, season the cavities of the trout with salt and pepper. Put the breadcrumbs into a bowl, add the parsley and chives, and toss gently. Fill the cavities of the trout with about ¼ cup of the breadcrumbs, pressing it in so that it doesn't fall out easily.

When the mushrooms are completely tender, squeeze in the juice of half a lemon, stir in the mustard, taste, and correct for salt and pepper.

Spread the mushrooms in a baking dish just big enough to hold the trout in a single layer. Set the trout on top of the mushrooms, drizzle the juice of half a lemon over them, and dot each fish with about 2 teaspoons of mustard butter.

Top the trout with the remaining breadcrumbs, set on the middle rack of the oven, and cook until the fish is just done, about 15 to 20 minutes.

Remove from the oven, cover with a sheet of aluminum foil, and let rest 10 to 15 minutes.

To serve, use a spatula to scoop up mushrooms, trout, and breadcrumbs in one motion and set on individual plates. Garnish with lemon wedges and enjoy right away.

Halibut Fillets
with Olive Mustard & Breadcrumbs

Serves 4 to 6

Halibut goes surprising well with red wine, especially cabernet sauvignon. Here, I've furthered a match with a good red wine by using olive mustard. For accompaniments, I recommend wild rice and sautéed chard. I originally developed this recipe for a weekly wine pairing column I write for the Santa Rosa Press Democrat; it has since become a favorite. If you don't have Olive Mustard and don't feel like making it, mix 6 tablespoons of Dijon mustard with 2 tablespoons of black olive tapenade.

2 pounds wild Pacific halibut fillet, cut into equal portions
Kosher salt
Black pepper in a mill
½ cup Olive Mustard, page 249, or Three Olive Mustard, page 250
1 cup Mustard Breadcrumbs, page 262
3 tablespoons butter

Set the halibut on a clean work surface and season it all over with salt and pepper. Use a pastry brush to coat it on both sides with mustard. Scatter breadcrumbs over the fish, press gently to make them stick, turn the fillets over, and repeat. Cover and let rest 10 minutes.

Set a large sauté pan over medium-high heat, add the butter, and when it is foamy, add the fillets. Sauté for 5 minutes, turn, and sauté 5 minutes more for 1-inch thick fillets. If the fish is thinner than one inch, cook for just 6 minutes. If thicker, cook for 12 minutes. Do not overcook; the fillets should turn opaque but remain juicy; the breadcrumbs should be golden brown.

Transfer the fillets to individual plates and serve immediately.

Grilled Tuna
with Black Beans, Pineapple & Serrano-Cilantro Mustard

Serves 6

Since I began writing about food in 1986, I have developed and published thousands of recipes. I remember, recognize, and understand them all, save one: This one. As I read through it, I have no memory of it, I have no idea what inspired it, and I have no memory of making it for the first time. It is my one Mystery Recipe. That said, it is also delicious, especially on a hot night. I've revised it just a bit, keeping its original spirit but editing it for the way I write and cook now. For a side dish, I recommend roasted, peeled, and seeded poblanos or Anaheim chilies, stuffed with a good grating cheese and heated in the oven until the cheese melts.

4 ounces black beans, soaked
    overnight in water to cover and
    drained
1 whole serrano, scored
1 small yellow onion
1 celery stalk, cut in half
4 garlic cloves, peeled
Kosher salt
Black pepper in a mill
Serrano–Cilantro Mustard, page 245

6 fresh ahi tuna steaks, about 6
    ounces each
½ fresh pineapple
6 fresh corn tortillas
Flake salt, such as Maldon Salt Flakes
    or Murray River Australian Salt
Black pepper in a mill
1 lime, cut in wedges
Sprigs of fresh cilantro

Put the beans in a heavy pot and add water to cover them by at least 2 inches. Add the serrano, onion, celery, and garlic cloves, set over high heat, and bring to a boil. Reduce the heat and simmer very gently until the beans are fully tender, about 45 minutes or a bit longer, depending on the age of the beans. Remove from the heat and use tongs to remove and discard the aromatics. Season with salt and pepper, set aside, and keep warm.

Set the tuna on a clean work surface, season all over with salt and pepper, and brush with mustard. Let sit for 30 minutes.

Meanwhile, peel the pineapple and remove its core. Cut half of it into very small dice and cut the other half into slices. Set aside.

Prepare a fire in a charcoal grill or preheat a broiler. Place the tuna steaks on the grill rack or on the broiler pan and cook until seared on the outside and still quite red in the center, about 3 to 4 minutes per side, at most.

While the tuna cooks, heat the tortillas over a flame or on a dry griddle until soft and hot; do not let them become crisp. Set them on individual warmed plates. Spoon hot black beans over each tortilla and top with a generous dollop of diced pineapple.

Working quickly, transfer the tuna to the plates, setting it off center on top of the beans. Top the tuna with a spoonful of mustard and a spoonful of pineapple. Add pineapple slices and a lime wedge to each plate. Season all over with salt and pepper and serve right away.

Chicken Breasts Marinated in Mustard Oil

with Radishes, Preserved Lemons & Orzo

Serves 4

Madeleine Kamman gets credit for this recipe, as I came across her version on a recipe flyer from a company in Napa Valley, now gone, promoting its mustard oil. I was drawn to the light and delicate flavors of the lemon and the radishes, and, after experimenting, added my own touch with orzo and preserved lemons, which I was making at the time. This is a delightfully refreshing dish, perfect on a hot summer day. If mustard oil is unavailable, use a delicate extra virgin olive oil, one from France or a late-harvest Ligurian oil, and add a tablespoon of white mustard seeds to the marinade.

Because chicken is best when cooked with its skin on the bone, this chicken must be handled very delicately or it will become hard and dry. Pull it off the heat before it is completely done; it will finish cooking and remain juicy and tender while it rests.

2 whole chicken breasts, boned, halved, skinned, and trimmed of all fat

1 clove garlic, crushed

6 tablespoons lemon juice

¾ cup mustard oil

Kosher salt

2 bunches fresh radishes, plus 4 small radishes, trimmed with stems on, for garnish

4 ounces seed-shaped pasta, such as orzo, riso, melone, rosemarina, or acini de pepi

Black pepper in a mill

2 tablespoons chopped radish leaves

3 slices preserved lemons, commercial or homemade, finely slivered, plus 4 slices for garnish, optional

Put the chicken breasts in a large, nonreactive dish. Whisk together the garlic, lemon juice, and mustard oil, season with salt, and spoon about half the mixture over the chicken. Set the remainder of the dressing aside. Cover and refrigerate the chicken, turning the breasts every hour or so for 3 to 4 hours.

Trim the radishes, reserving the pert leaves, slice them ⅛-inch thick, and hold them in ice water until ready to use. Chop the radish leaves; you should have about 2 tablespoons.

Remove the chicken from the refrigerator 30 minutes before finishing the dish.

Cook the pasta according to package directions. Drain, transfer to a wide shallow bowl, toss with 1 tablespoon of the dressing, and keep warm.

Pour the marinade from the chicken into a heavy sauté pan and set it over medium heat. Season the chicken all over with salt and pepper, set it in the pan in a single layer, and cook, turning every 2 minutes or so, until it has just barely firmed up, about 8 minutes. Remove from the heat, cover, and keep warm.

Drain the radishes, return the pan to medium heat, add about a tablespoon of the reserved dressing, and sauté the radishes for about 2 minutes, until they turn bright red. Season with salt and pepper and remove from the heat.

Stir the chopped radish leaves and slivered preserved lemons into the reserved dressing.

Spoon warm pasta onto individual plates and add chicken, draping it partially on and partially off the pasta. Add sautéed radishes alongside, spoon dressing over everything, garnishing with a whole radish and a slice of preserved lemon, and season with a few turns of black pepper. Serve right away.

Chicken Legs Baked in Mustard

Serves 4

It can be a challenge to get a great dinner on the table during the week, and this recipe can help. If you have the breadcrumbs on hand, it takes just minutes of hands-on work to prepare it.

½ cup Dijon mustard
3 garlic cloves, pressed, plus 2 cloves
    garlic, minced
2 teaspoons soy sauce
1 teaspoon dried thyme leaves,
    crushed

3 tablespoons olive oil
4 pastured chicken leg-thighs
1 cup Mustard Breadcrumbs,
    page 262

Preheat the oven to 375 degrees.

Put the mustard, pressed and minced garlic, soy sauce, thyme and olive oil into a small bowl and whisk thoroughly. Coat the chicken in the mixture, roll it in breadcrumbs, and set on a rack in a roasting pan.

Set on the middle rack of the oven and cook until the chicken reaches an internal temperature of about 155 degrees in its thickest part, about 35 to 40 minutes.

Remove from the oven, let rest 10 or 15 minutes, and serve.

Serving Suggestions: with steamed rice and wilted spinach; with oven-roasted potatoes and grilled zucchini; or with Spicy Glazed Carrots, page 200.

Variation:
- To make this dish with duck, use Honey-Pepper Mustard, Honey-Ginger Mustard, or a commercial fruit mustard. Bake for about 90 minutes.

Chicken Dijonnaise

Serves 4

The dish comes from mustard's heartland, Dijon itself. Its preparation is featured in the film Spice of Life *and, although a specific recipe is not given, I believe this version captures the spirit if not the letter of the recipe named in honor of Madame Gaston Gerard, wife of a former mayor of Dijon. The inclusion of cheese in the sauce is said to be her inspiration; the whole cloves of garlic are my contribution.*

4 pastured chicken leg-thigh pieces or 1 roasting chicken, 4 to 5 pounds, cut in pieces, rinsed, and patted dry
Kosher salt
Black pepper in a mill
2 cups, approximately, buttermilk
1 tablespoon butter
1 tablespoon olive oil
5 or 6 cloves garlic
¾ cup dry white wine
2 cups heavy cream
4 tablespoons Dijon mustard
5 ounces Gruyère cheese, grated
4 tablespoons fresh Italian parsley, minced
1 cup Mustard Breadcrumbs, page 262

Several hours before cooking the chicken, season it all over with salt and pepper and put it into a bowl or other container that will hold it snugly in a single layer. Pour the buttermilk over it and refrigerate; bring to room temperature before continuing.

Preheat the oven to 325 degrees.

Melt the butter in a large sauté pan or skillet set over medium heat, add the olive oil, and sauté the garlic cloves, turning them frequently, until they begin to soften, about 6 to 7 minutes; do not let them burn. Remove them from the pan and set aside.

Remove the chicken from the buttermilk and dry with a paper towel. Add the chicken to the pan and cook, turning once or twice, until it is golden brown all over. Transfer the chicken to a baking dish that will hold it snugly in a single layer and set on the middle rack of the oven; cook for 20 minutes.

Meanwhile, return the pan to medium heat, add the sautéed garlic and the wine, and deglaze the pan. Simmer until the wine is nearly completely reduced and the garlic is very soft. Use a fork to mash the garlic, add the cream, and simmer gently until it is reduced by one third. Stir in the mustard and remove from the heat. Add half the cheese and half the parsley and stir gently until the cheese is melted.

Taste the sauce and correct for salt and pepper.

Pull the chicken from the oven, pour the sauce over it, and top with the remaining cheese, the remaining parsley, and the breadcrumbs.

Set under a broiler or in a very hot oven until the cheese melts and the breadcrumbs take on a bit of color.

Let the chicken rest for 5 to 10 minutes before serving.

Serving Suggestions: Serve with steamed rice or roasted new potatoes and wilted spinach or sautéed chard.

Chicken
with Soft Polenta & Mustard Greens

Serves 4

Both chicken and polenta are staples in my kitchen and I often serve them together, sometimes with the chicken slathered with mustard, as in this dish. Because both the polenta and the chicken serve as canvases, so to speak, for other flavors, this is a great dish for experimenting with flavored mustards. Maille, for example, makes a lovely apricot, curry spice and white wine mustard that would be lovely with this dish, especially when you add grilled apricots alongside. If you love mushrooms, stir a spoonful of Maille Morel & Chablis Mustard into the polenta and use it on the chicken, too. When you have fresh tarragon in your garden, use Fallot's Tarragon Mustard on the chicken and finish the dish with a shower of the fresh herb.

1 chicken, about 4 pounds, cut into pieces
Olive oil
Kosher salt
Black pepper in a mill
1 lemon
4 tablespoons mustard of choice, optional

1 cup polenta
2 tablespoons butter
¾ cup (3 ounces) grated Parmigiano-Reggiano or similar cheese
1 bunch mustard greens, trimmed and cut into ½-inch wide strips
2 garlic cloves, pressed

Rub the chicken with olive oil and season all over with salt and pepper. Squeeze the juice of the lemon over the chicken and let rest for an hour.

Preheat the oven to 400 degrees.

If using the mustard, brush it over the chicken.

Put the chicken on a rack in a roasting pan and bake for 40 to 50 minutes, until cooked through but still juicy.

Meanwhile, pour 3 cups of water into a medium saucepan and bring to a boil over high heat. Using a whisk, stir the water in one direction to create a vortex; slowly pour the polenta into the vortex, whisking all the while.

A Mustard Cookbook

Continue to stir until the polenta thickens. Season with salt, reduce the heat to low, and simmer gently until the polenta is completely tender. Add more water as needed if the polenta becomes too thick; it should be loose enough to drop from a spoon. It will take 20 to 40 minutes for the polenta to cook, depending on the age and size of the grains. When the polenta is almost done, stir in the butter and cheese, taste, and season with salt and pepper. Keep over very low heat until ready to serve.

About 10 minutes before the chicken is ready, pour a little olive oil into a sauté pan set over medium heat, add the mustard greens, and sauté, turning frequently, until limp and tender. Add the pressed garlic, season with salt and pepper, cover the pan, and remove from the heat.

Remove the chicken from the oven, cover, and let rest 5 to 10 minutes.

To serve, ladle polenta into soup plates, add chicken and mustard greens, and serve right away.

Chicken Stew
with Winter Squash & Mustard Greens

Serves 4 as a main course; 8 as a first course

Here is a perfect rainy day dish, full of warm spices and rich textures.

3 tablespoons olive oil
8 chicken thighs, bone in, preferably from pastured chickens

Kosher salt
Black Pepper in a mill
2 red onions, cut into ½-inch squares
8 cloves garlic, minced
2 serranos, minced
¼ teaspoon ground nutmeg
¼ teaspoon ground cardamom
½ teaspoon ground cumin
1 cup cooked chickpeas
1 cup unpeeled waxy potatoes, in ½-inch cubes
1 cup butternut or similar winter squash, in ½-inch cubes
6 cups homemade chicken stock
8 ounces mustard greens, trimmed and cut into ½-inch wide strips
¼ cup chopped cilantro leaves

Heat 2 tablespoons of the olive oil in a large, heavy pot. Season the chicken all over with salt and pepper and sauté until golden brown all over. Transfer the chicken from the pot to a plate.

Add the onions to the pot and sauté until transparent. Add the garlic and serranos and sauté 2 minutes more. Add the spices, chickpeas, potatoes, and squash, sauté 2 minutes, add the chicken stock, and return the chicken to the pot. Simmer until the potatoes and squash are just tender and the chicken is cooked through, about 15 to 20 minutes.

Meanwhile, sauté the mustard greens in the remaining tablespoon of olive oil until they are just limp. Add the greens to the soup. Taste, and adjust seasoning with salt and pepper.

To serve as a main course, put 2 pieces of chicken into individual soup bowls and ladle the broth and vegetables on top. To serve as a first course, put 1 piece of chicken into individual soup plates and ladle broth and vegetables on top.

Sprinkle with cilantro and serve right away.

Seared Duck Breast
with Cranberry-Mustard Sauce

Serves 3 to 4

In the first edition of this book, I offered a recipe for roasted duckling with cranberry-mustard sauce because it was not easy, in the early 1990s, for home cooks to acquire quality duck breast in many parts of the United States. It is much easier to get it now and it produces fabulous results, with rich succulent meat—rare!—beautifully accented by the tangy mustard. If you don't have cranberry mustard, use commercial Black Currant Mustard from France. Glazed carrots make a perfect side dish.

1 whole duck breast
1 teaspoon ground allspice
1 teaspoon ground cloves
1 tablespoon grated orange zest
Kosher salt
Black pepper in a mill
½ cup dry red wine

1 shallot, minced
½ cup Cranberry-Mustard Sauce, (see below)
Zest of 1 orange
3 tablespoons butter
Orange wedges, for garnish
Thyme sprigs, for garnish

Divide the duck breast, if still joined, into two pieces and set on a work surface. Trim the skin so that none hangs over the meat. Score the skin diagonally, with cuts about 1 inch apart. Score in the other direction, creating a patchwork of squares; be sure to cut *to* and not through the meat.

In a small bowl, combine the allspice, cloves, and orange zest. Add 2 teaspoons of salt and several generous turns of black pepper. Rub the mixture over the duck; cover and let rest 30 minutes.

Set a heavy ridged pan—cast iron is ideal—over high heat and when it is hot, add the duck, skin side down, and cook for 4 to 5 minutes, until the skin is golden brown and crisp. Turn and cook 2 minutes more for rare and 3 minutes more for medium rare; do not cook beyond medium rare.

Transfer to a warm plate, skin side up, cover with aluminum foil, and let rest 5 minutes.

While the duck rests, make the sauce.

With the pan over high heat, add the wine and swirl the pan to deglaze it. Transfer the liquid to a small saucepan, add the shallot, and simmer until it softens. Stir in the mustard sauce and orange zest, heat through, add the butter, taste, and correct for salt and pepper. Swirl the pan to incorporate the butter and remove from the heat.

Use a sharp knife to cut the duck into thin diagonal slices and set on warmed plates. Spoon sauce over it, add accompaniments, garnish with orange wedges and thyme sprigs, and serve right away.

Rabbit Dijonnaise

Serves 3 to 4

Many Americans have a strong prejudice against eating rabbit. It is a sentimental aversion, based on the rabbit's appearance. Yet it is an excellent source of protein and has a small carbon footprint; it was once raised on nearly every family farm in the country. Today, it is making a comeback and you can find it at farmers' markets and grocery stores such as Whole Foods. There are many versions of this classic French dish and this one happens to be my favorite. It is nearly identical to Chicken Dijonnaise. I like to serve it with simple roasted potatoes, as their earthy simplicity is ideal with the sauce.

1 3-pound rabbit, dressed and cut
    into 6 pieces (see note below)
Kosher salt
Black pepper in a mill
3 tablespoons butter
6 garlic cloves, peeled
½ cup dry white wine
1 cup chicken stock

¾ cup heavy cream
¾ cup crème fraîche
4 tablespoons Dijon mustard
5 ounces Gruyère cheese, grated
4 tablespoons minced fresh Italian
    parsley
1 cup Mustard Breadcrumbs,
    page 262

Rinse the rabbit under cool tap water, pat dry with a tea towel, and season all over with salt and pepper.

Put the butter and olive oil in a heavy skillet set over medium-low heat and when the butter melts, add the garlic and sauté, turning frequently, until they just begin to pick up some color. Use tongs to transfer the garlic to a bowl or plate.

Sauté the rabbit for 2 to 3 minutes, turn, and saute 2 to 3 minutes more or until golden brown. Add the white wine and chicken stock and when the liquid boils, reduce the heat to very low, cover the skillet, and simmer very gently for 10 minutes, or until the rabbit is just cooked through.

Preheat the oven to 200 degrees.

Transfer the rabbit to a baking dish that will hold it in a single layer. Cover and set in the oven to keep warm.

A Mustard Cookbook

Working quickly, increase the heat under the skillet to high, return the garlic to the pan, and simmer the cooking juices until they are reduced to about ½ cup. Use a fork to mash the garlic into a smooth puree.

Add the cream and crème fraîche and cook until it is reduced by one third. Stir in the mustard, half the cheese, and half the parsley and remove from the heat.

If the stove has a broiler, turn it on high. If there is no broiler, increase the oven heat to 475 degrees.

Remove the rabbit from the oven and pour the sauce over it. Top with the remaining cheese, the parsley, and the breadcrumbs. Set under the broiler or in the hot oven until the cheese melts and the breadcrumbs are just picking up some color.

Remove from the oven and let rest 5 minutes before serving.

NOTE

The very best way to learn to carve a rabbit is to have your butcher or rabbit purveyor show you. It is not hard but it can be difficult to visualize if you've not done it before. I'll do my best to explain. First, set the rabbit on its back on a clean work surface. Grasp a hind leg with one hand and with the other carve where the leg joins the body, cutting inward to separate the thigh from the tail bone. Grasp a foreleg with one hand and with the other, cut along the neck bone to separate the leg. Turn the rabbit over and repeat on the other side.

Next, use your fingers to find the rib bones nearest the tail; cut between the second and third rib to release the two flaps of meat on either side of the saddle. Use a cleaver to cut the rib cage from the saddle and flaps; be sure to cut all the way through the backbone. Cut the tailbone from the salad and reserve both the rib cage and tailbone for making stock. Use the cleaver to cut the saddle in half lengthwise, cutting through the backbone and make a crosswise cut to separate the saddle into quarters.

Rack of Lamb Dijonnaise

Serves 2, easily doubled

I've always thought of rack of lamb as one of the perfect romantic dinners (along with Steak au Poivre and fresh Dungeness crab), especially with a beautiful Russian River Valley or French pinot noir alongside. Yet because the recipe is so easy, it is a simple matter to increase it.

½ lamb rack (4 ribs), preferably
    American lamb
Kosher salt
Black pepper in a mill

⅓ cup Dijon mustard
¾ cup Mustard Breadcrumbs, page 262
Mustard flowers, chive flowers, or
    snipped chives, for garnish

Preheat the oven to 300 degrees.

Season the lamb all over with salt and pepper.

Set a heavy skillet—cast iron is perfect—over high heat and, when the pan is very hot, sear the skin side of the rack. Turn the lamb skin side up, transfer to the oven, and cook for 20 minutes.

Remove from the oven and increase the oven heat to 375 degrees.

Brush the lamb with Dijon, apply it fairly heavily. Press breadcrumbs into the flesh and sprinkle them over the skin, as well.

Return to the oven and cook for 10 minutes; test the temperature and, if it is below 125 degrees (for rare) or 135 degrees (for medium rare), cook 5 to 10 minutes more.

Remove from the oven, cover with a sheet of aluminum foil, and let rest for 10 minutes, during which time its temperature will continue to rise.

Slice the rack into four separate chops, set on warmed plates, add accompaniments, and serve right away.

Serving Suggestions: with parsnip puree, page 166; with roasted potatoes, page 202; with gratin of potatoes, page 204, and a green vegetable, such as poached leeks, oven-roasted asparagus, wilted spinach, or braised mustard mustard greens.

To drink: A suave, delicate pinot noir, one that is not over-extracted or too high in alcohol; sparkling wine, especially a dry sparkling rosé, is also a good choice.

Oven-Roasted Leg of Lamb
with Sausage Stuffing & Mustard Glaze

Serves 6 to 8

This is the first recipe I ever published, long ago in a column entitled, "Try Lamb for Easter." It appears here with very few alterations, and is as delicious now as it was then, festive and perfect for a special occasion. Use American lamb, preferably from a small producer. When you make this during the spring, try to find some mustard flowers to use both as garnish and as a bouquet for the table.

1 leg of lamb, boned and butterflied, about 5 pounds
Olive oil
1 small yellow onion, chopped
5 garlic cloves, minced
1 pound bulk Italian sausage
2 tablespoons Dijon mustard

1 teaspoon fresh thyme leaves
1 teaspoon fresh summer savory leaves
1 teaspoon minced fresh rosemary
1 cup fresh breadcrumbs
1 tablespoon butter
Fresh herb sprigs, for garnish

Mustard Glaze

¾ cup Dijon mustard
½ cup pure olive oil
1 teaspoon fresh thyme leaves

1 teaspoon fresh summer savory leaves
½ teaspoon fresh rosemary, minced

Remove the papery outer covering of the lamb (the fell), the silver skin, and any large strips of fat. Set the meat aside.

Heat a small amount of the olive oil in a heavy skillet over medium heat and sauté the onions until soft and transparent, about 10 minutes. Add the garlic and sauté for another 2 minutes. Add the sausage, crumble it with a fork, and cook until it is about half-done. Stir in the mustard and fresh herbs. Add the breadcrumbs and toss. Remove from the heat and set aside briefly to cool a bit.

While the stuffing cools, make the glaze. To do so, put the mustard, olive oil, thyme, summer savory, and rosemary in a small bowl, whisk, taste, and season with salt and pepper. Set aside.

Preheat the oven to 400 degrees.

Place the boned leg of lamb, outside down, on a flat working surface. Season it with salt and pepper and brush with some of the glaze. Spread the filling over the meat, roll it into a loaf, tucking pieces as necessary, and tie it tightly with kitchen twine.

Put the lamb on a rack in a roasting pan, brush it all over with glaze, and set on the middle rack of the oven. Cook for 15 minutes, lower the heat to 350 degrees, and cook for about 15 minutes per pound, until the center temperature reaches 135 degrees.

Remove from the heat, transfer to a warm platter, cover with a sheet of aluminum foil, and let rest 20 minutes.

Meanwhile, set the roasting pan over medium heat, add a cup of water, and deglaze the pan. Simmer until the liquid is reduced to just 3 tablespoons. Stir in the remaining marinade, heat through, add the butter, taste, and correct for salt and pepper. Tip the sauce into a serving bowl or small pitcher. Keep warm.

To serve, cut the lamb into ⅜-inch thick slices, arrange on a platter, and garnish with herb sprigs. Serve right away, with the sauce alongside.

Lamb's Tongue
in Saffron-Mustard Cream
with Forbidden Rice

Serves 4 to 6

    One of the most delicious things I have ever tasted anywhere is a simple dish of lamb's tongue in a sour-cream and saffron sauce, served at Meykadeh, a Persian restaurant in San Francisco's North Beach. For years, I drove there to enjoy it but eventually lamb's tongue became available at local farmers' markets and specialty butcher shops and so I began making my own. This version is inspired by the restaurant's but not identical, as I have added beautiful black rice to make it a full meal.

8 to 10 lamb's tongues
Kosher salt
1 bay leaf
2 allspice berries
1 whole clove
1 teaspoon white peppercorns
1 cup forbidden black rice, rinsed in
    two or three changes of water
    and drained

Boiling water
1 cup Saffron Mustard Cream,
    page 221
Juice of 1 lime
Black pepper in a mill
1 teaspoon za'atar (see note below)

Rinse the lamb's tongues under cool water and set them on a tea towel.

Fill a medium saucepan half full with water, add a generous tablespoon of salt, along with the bay leaf, allspice, clove, and peppercorns. Stir and add the tongue.

Bring to a boil over high heat and when the water boils, reduce the heat so that it simmers gently. Cook until the tongues are very tender, about 1 ¼ hours or a bit longer. Turn off the heat and let the tongues cool in the cooking liquid. When they are cool enough to handle but not cold, transfer them one at a time and remove the white skin, which should pull off easily with your fingers. Put the peeled tongue back into the liquid and keep warm.

While the tongue is cooking, prepare the rice. Fill a deep steamer with about 2 to 3 inches of water. Put the rice into a deep bowl that will fit inside the steamer, add a pinch of salt, and pour in enough boiling water to completely cover the rice; you should be able to see the water a bit above the rice itself. Set this bowl into the steamer, cover the pot, and cook until the rice is tender, about 50 minutes. Begin checking the rice after 30 minutes, as cooking times can vary widely based on the age of the rice. When the rice is tender, turn off the heat and let the rice rest in the steamer.

Transfer the tongue to a clean work surface and cut each one into ¾-inch chunks and put them into a medium mixing bowl, season with salt and pepper, and toss gently.

Stir the Saffron Mustard Cream to loosen it slightly, add the lime juice, taste, correct for salt, and season with several generous turns of black pepper.

Pour about three-quarters of the sauce over the tongue and toss gently.

To serve, set a generous scoop of rice onto individual plates, using colors that will set off its black color. Top with tongue and sprinkle each portion with a little za'atar.

Serve immediately, with the remaining sauce on the side.

NOTE
Za'atar is a mixture of sumac, sesame seeds, salt, and usually thyme and oregano. It is a common condiment in the Middle East and has a bright tangy flavor, not unlike lemon.

Poached Lamb & Goat Meat Loaf
with Parsnip Puree

Serves 6

Poaching creates a succulent meatloaf, with a voluptuous richness, yet this recipe makes a good oven-roasted meatloaf, too. You'll find instructions following the main recipe. For goat meat, check your local farmers' market; it is increasingly common throughout the US.

2 tablespoons olive oil, lard, or butter
1 large yellow onion, cut into small dice
6 garlic cloves, minced
Kosher salt
1 pound ground lamb
1 pound ground goat
3 tablespoons Dijon mustard
1 large pastured egg, beaten
1 cup dried (not toasted) breadcrumbs or steamed quinoa
¼ cup chopped fresh flat-leaf parsley
1 tablespoon crushed black peppercorns

½ teaspoons ground allspice
Black pepper in a mill
6 ounces blue cheese, such as Point Reyes Original Blue, in small cubes
6 cups homemade meat stock, hot
2 pounds parsnips, trimmed, peeled, and cut into cubes
1 russet potato, peeled and cut into cubes
4 tablespoons butter, at room temperature
3 tablespoons crème fraîche or heavy cream, plus more as needed

Put the fat into a sauté pan set over medium heat, add the onion and sauté until soft and fragrant, about 12 to 15 minutes. Add the garlic and sauté 2 minutes more. Season with salt; remove from the heat and set aside.

Put the meats into a medium mixing bowl. Add the mustard, egg, breadcrumbs, parsley, peppercorns, and allspice. Add the cooled onion and garlic and mix thoroughly.

Season with several turns of black pepper and a generous few pinches of salt and mix again. Fold in the blue cheese and mix lightly, leaving cubes whole.

Turn the mixture onto a work surface and form a roll about 3 ½ to 4 inches in diameter. Wrap the roll in a double layer of cheesecloth and use kitchen twine to tie it on both ends.

Set a fish poacher or similar container over two medium-high burners and pour in the hot stock. Carefully lower the meatloaf into the liquid and add the parsnips and potatoes. If the meatloaf is not fully covered, add water.

When the liquid boils, reduce the heat to low and simmer very gently for 40 minutes.

Turn off the heat and use a wide slotted spoon to transfer the potatoes and parsnips to a bowl. Cover the pot, and let the meatloaf rest for 45 minutes.

Meanwhile, pass the parsnips and potatoes through a food mill or potato ricer into a medium saucepan. Add the butter, about a tablespoon at a time, and whip well between additions. Add the crème fraîche or cream, taste, and season with salt and pepper. If the mixture seems a bit too thick, add more crème fraîche or cream. Cover and keep warm.

Remove the meatloaf from the stock, set on a rack over a plate or pan, and let drain while you reheat the parsnips over very low heat. Cut the ends of the cheesecloth, unwrap the meatloaf, and cut it into ½-inch rounds.

Divide the parsnip puree among individual plates, add the meatloaf alongside, and drizzle with just a bit of the poaching liquid. Serve right away.

NOTE
To cook the meatloaf in the oven, omit the cheesecloth and pack the mixture into a loaf pan and bake in a 350 degree oven for about 50 to 60 minutes, until cooked through. Remove from the oven, cover with a sheet of aluminum foil, and let rest 10 to 15 minutes before slicing and serving.

Southern-Style Mustard Greens & Ham Hocks
with New Potatoes

Generally served as a side dish with fried or roasted chicken, ham, or black-eyed peas, I find greens and ham hocks also makes a great main course, especially when accompanied by corn bread. It is best in the cooler months, not only because it is hearty and warming, but because that's when mustard greens are at their best. Brassicas thrive in cool weather.

3 ham hocks, split
4 large bunches of mustard greens
2½ pounds small new potatoes, scrubbed and halved

Black pepper in a mill
Kosher salt
¼ cup apple cider vinegar
¼ cup Tabasco sauce

Put the ham hocks in a large soup pot and add 12 cups (3 quarts) water. Bring to a boil over high heat, skim off the foam that forms on the surface, reduce the heat, and simmer gently for 1½ hours, removing additional foam as it forms.

Meanwhile, trim the greens, removing any tough stems and yellowed leaves. Soak them briefly in warm water and transfer to absorbent paper or a tea towel.

Slice the greens into crosswise inch-wide strips. Add the greens and the potatoes to the ham hocks and cook 20 to 25 minutes; younger greens will cook more quickly than older, mature greens.

Use tongs to lift out the ham hocks and set them aside until cool enough to handle. Pull the meat off the bone and remove the marrow, if any. Discard the bones and stir the meat and marrow into the pot. Test a potato or two to be sure they are tender.

Season with several very generous turns of black pepper; taste and correct for salt, as needed.

Combine the vinegar and Tabasco sauce in a small bowl and add 2 tablespoons to the pot. Ladle into soup bowls, being certain that each portion has potatoes, greens, and meat. Serve right away, with the remaining vinegar sauce alongside.

A Mustard Cookbook

Pork Loin
with Apricot-Mustard Glaze

Serves 4

Pork and apricots are one of the great culinary marriages, especially from mid-May through mid-June, when apricots are in season. At other times, omit the apricots rather than buy those from the Southern Hemisphere, which lack true apricot flavor. In this simple but elegant example, the mustard adds another dimension. Grilled or braised fennel or sautéed zucchini make excellent side dishes.

½ cup apricot jam
3 tablespoons Dijon mustard or
    coarse-grain mustard
1 cup white wine

1 pork tenderloin, about 1½ pounds
1 pound apricots
Salt and freshly ground black pepper

Put the jam, mustard, and ½ cup of the white wine into a small bowl and stir well. Put the pork into a freezer bag, add about ⅔ of jam mixture, seal the bag, pressing out the air as you do, and seal it. Massage the pork a bit to completely coat it in the sauce. Refrigerate for at least 1 hour and as long as overnight. Remove from the refrigerator 30 minutes before cooking.

Preheat the oven to 350 degrees. Remove the pork from the bag, set it on a rack in a small roasting pan, and cook until it reaches an internal temperature of about 155 degrees, about 15 to 20 minutes.

Working quickly, cut the apricots in half, remove their stones, and brush the cut sides with a bit of the remaining marinade. Set them, cut sides up, in a small oven-proof pan and set in the oven, alongside the pork, about 5 minutes before it is done. Remove the pork from the oven, transfer to a warm plate, cover with aluminum foil, and let rest about 10 minutes.

Set the roasting pan over a medium flame, deglaze the pan with the remaining wine, stir in the remaining marinade, and simmer gently until the sauce is reduced by half. Season to taste with salt and pepper and remove from the heat.

Cut the pork into thin slices and arrange on warm plates; add the apricots and other accompaniments, spoon sauce on top, and serve right away.

Slow-Roasted Pork Shoulder
with Mustards & Herbs

Serves 6 to 8

Slow-cooked pork shoulder is one of the most delicious meats there is, especially when made with a heritage breed pig. If you can't find a heritage breed, try to get your pork at a farmers' market so that you'll know it was raised close to home. Commodity pork has a harmful effect on the environment and pigs raised in huge factory farms live miserable lives.

I prepare this version in the fall and winter, when sage is the herb of the season. For other seasonal ideas, consult the variations that follow the recipe.

1 pork shoulder, bone-in, about 5 pounds, preferably a heritage breed

Kosher salt

Black Pepper in a mill

⅓ cup Dijon mustard, plus more for serving

⅓ cup Old Style (coarse-grain) Dijon mustard, plus more for serving

2 large yellow onions, trimmed, peeled and cut into ¼-inch-thick rounds

7 or 8 garlic cloves, peeled

1 bay leaf

2 or 3 Italian parsley sprigs

2 or 3 large sage sprigs

3 tablespoons chopped fresh sage

Set the pork on a clean work surface and season it all over with salt and pepper. Rub the pork all over with the Dijon mustard, being certain to rub it into all the crevices. Spread the coarse-grain mustard all over it, too. Set aside briefly.

Spread the onions over the surface of a deep clay pot or Dutch oven and season lightly with salt. Scatter the garlic cloves on top and add the parsley and sage sprigs. Add water to come up the side of the pot by ¼ inch. Set the pork on top.

Cover the pot with its lid or a sheet of aluminum pinched tightly so it stays in place and set on the middle rack of the oven. Set the temperature to 275 degrees.

Cook for 2 hours, uncover, and carefully spoon some of the cooking juices over the meat. Cover and continue to cook until the meat falls apart easily when pressed, about 4 to 5 hours. Baste with juices every hour or so.

Remove from the oven, leave covered, and let rest from 15 to 30 minutes while you prepare accompaniments.

To serve, tear the pork into pieces with two forks or hack it into chunks with a cleaver. Pour the pan juices into a gravy cup and drizzle them over the meat, leaving the fat behind. Discard the aromatics.

Garnish the pork with chopped sage and serve right away.

Serving Suggestions: with creamy polenta or grits; with roasted potatoes; with steamed brown rice; with roasted or sautéed winter squash; with grilled cabbage wedges.

To Drink: A sour craft beer from a small domestic producer or a dry hard cider.

Variations:

- In the spring, replace the onions with leeks (white and pale green parts only, thoroughly cleaned, sliced in ¼-inch rounds) and spring garlic. Omit the sage, add chervil sprigs and chives, and top with fresh snipped chives. Instead of water, use dry white wine as the liquid.

- In the summer, add roasted and peeled chilies, such as poblanos, Gypsy peppers, or New Mexico chiles, cut into wide julienne. Add 2 or 3 serranos, julienned, and a pint of small cherry tomatoes, stems removed; omit the sage. Add the juice of 2 to 3 limes to the water in the pan. After draining the pan juices, use a slotted spoon to transfer the vegetables to the serving platter. Toss together 2 tablespoons chopped fresh cilantro and 2 tablespoons chopped fresh basil and scatter over the meat immediately before serving. Set the pork on top of the vegetables, scatter the herbs on top, and serve with lime wedges.

Baby Back Ribs

Serves 4

These ribs are tender, just slightly sweet, and full of the subtle aroma of ginger, garlic, and mustard. This is a balanced marinade, in which each ingredient plays a crucial role but none dominates. In testing this recipe, I found that the longer the ribs marinated, the more delicate was the flavor, so give it as much time as you can. These ribs are delicious on their own, but certainly serve additional sweet coarse-grain mustard on the side if you wish. Accompany with coleslaw, potato salad, or steamed jasmine rice.

For the marinade:

½ cup coarse-grain mustard
½ cup firmly packed brown sugar
3 tablespoons minced garlic
3 tablespoons grated fresh ginger

3 shallots, minced
½ cup rice vinegar
1 cup soy sauce

4 to 5 pounds baby back ribs, in slabs

Put the mustard, brown sugar, garlic, ginger, and shallots into a bowl, add the vinegar and soy sauce and stir, until the sugar dissolves. Rub each slab of ribs with the marinade, place them in a shallow pan, and pour the rest of the marinade over them. Cover and marinate the ribs for at least 24 hours or for up to 72 hours.

Prepare a fire in a charcoal grill or preheat an oven to 400 degrees. Grill the ribs over the hot coals or in the oven until they are cooked through and tender, about 25 to 30 minutes. Turn now and then and be certain not to let them burn.

Transfer to a platter and serve right away.

Variations:

1. Use chicken drummettes (the meaty part of the wing) instead of ribs. Marinate the chicken for 24 hours. Place the drummettes in a baking dish (do not crowd them) and bake at 325°F for 40 minutes.

2. Marinate slices or cubes of pork for 24 hours, thread on skewers with wedges of onion and fresh pineapple, and grill or broil. Serve with jasmine rice and a spicy mustard sauce for dipping.

Ham Steaks

with Red-Eye Gravy and Grits

Serves 4

Serve this luscious ham for breakfast, with biscuits and fried eggs alongside, or for supper, with potatoes, grits, or polenta and some sort of braised or wilted greens.

3 tablespoons butter

2 large ham steaks, preferably center cut, halved

1 cup strong brewed coffee

2 tablespoon Dijon mustard, coarse-grain mustard, or other mustard of choice, plus more to taste

1 tablespoon maple syrup, molasses, or honey, plus more to taste

Generous pinch crushed red pepper flakes

Kosher salt

Black pepper in a mill

Preheat the oven to 250 degrees.

In a large heavy skillet set over medium heat, melt a tablespoon of the butter, and, when it is melted, add 2 pieces of ham. Sauté 2 minutes, turn, and sauté 2 minutes more. Transfer to a plate and set in the warm oven. Repeat with the other 2 pieces of ham.

Return the skillet to medium heat, add the coffee, and deglaze the pan. Stir in the mustard and syrup, molasses, or honey, along with the crushed red pepper flakes. Taste for balance and sweetness, adding a bit more mustard or a bit more sweetener, as needed. Simmer until the mixture reduces slightly. Taste and season with salt and pepper.

Swirl in the butter and the moment it melts, remove the pan from the heat.

Working quickly, transfer the ham to individual plates, spoon sauce on top, and serve immediately.

Country Ham
with Red-Eye Gravy

Serves 10 to 12

I have been intrigued by the thought of combining coffee and mustard since I read M. F. K. Fisher's comment about Frederick the Great's habit of doing so. He made his coffee with Champagne instead of water, she tells us in Serve It Forth, *and then stirred in powdered mustard to make the flavors stronger.*

"Now to me it seems improbable that Frederick truly liked this brew," Fisher comments. "I suspect him of bravado. Or perhaps he was taste-blind."

Today, we might say he was a "non-taster," one of three categories of taste based on the number of taste-buds an individual possesses. Hyper-tasters have the most tastebuds, tasters an average number, and non-tasters the fewest; non-tasters can tolerate higher levels of bitterness.

Of course, mustard and coffee are combined in other ways, including in a traditional recipe, popular in the American Midwest and South, "red-eye gravy." There are many versions, all with coffee and only some, especially those from Alabama and surrounding areas, with mustard.

The best dry-cured country hams require long soaking and simmering, but the results are well worth the effort. If you use another type of ham, simply omit the step for soaking it and bake it, as you typically would, in the oven.

1 cured ham, 7 to 8 pound
2 yellow onions, quartered
1 head of garlic, cut in half
3 bay leaves
1 tablespoon black peppercorns
3 cups apple cider vinegar, medium acid

3 cups brewed black coffee, preferably French press method
1 cup brown sugar, firmly packed
1 cup mustard, either prepared brown or Dijon
Kosher salt
Black pepper in a mill

Set the ham in a large container, cover with cold water, and let soak for 24 hours. Transfer to a clean work surface and scrub off any mold that may have formed on the skin. If you want to be certain the ham isn't too salty, soak in fresh water for another day.

Drain.

Put the ham in a large soup pot, add the onion, garlic, bay, and peppercorns and bring to a boil over high heat. Reduce the heat, skim off any foam that rises to the surface, and simmer gently for 15 minutes per pound. Halfway through, add the vinegar.

Shortly before the ham is ready, pour the coffee into a small saucepan, add the sugar, set over low heat, and whisk until the sugar melts. Stir in mustard and remove from the heat. Taste and season with salt and pepper as needed.

Preheat the oven to 400 degrees.

Transfer the ham from the kettle to the rack of a roasting pan and carefully remove the skin and trim the fat, leaving just ¼ inch of fat on the ham. Brush the ham with the coffee glaze and set it in the oven. Baste the ham with glaze every 15 minutes and bake the ham for about 1 hour, or until it reaches an internal temperature of 160 degrees.

Remove the ham from the oven, transfer to a platter, and place the roasting pan over medium heat. Add the remaining coffee glaze to the roasting pan, deglaze the pan, scraping up any particles, and reduce the glaze by about one half, until it is the consistency of a thin syrup. Carve the ham, slicing it very thinly, and serve it immediately with the sauce alongside.

Polenta
with Sausages, Apples & Mustard Greens

Serves 4 to 6

When I make this dish in the spring, I decorate my table with a bouquet of mustard flowers and apple blossoms, which I pick a few steps from my kitchen. If you don't have these, any spring flower will do.

1 cup polenta
Kosher salt
5 teaspoons hot mustard flour, mixed with 2 tablespoons water
2 pounds chicken-apple sausages or other sausages of choice
3 cups white wine of choice
4 tablespoons butter

3½ ounces dry Jack or similar cheese, grated
2 tart-sweet apples, peeled, cored, and cut into ¼-inch-thick rounds
1 bunch young mustard greens, trimmed and rinsed

Put 4 cups of the water in a large saucepan, season generously with salt and bring to a boil over high heat. When the water boils, stir it with a whisk, always moving in the same direction to create a vortex. Slowly pour the polenta into the vortex and continue to whisk until the mixture returns to a boil and begins to thicken. Lower the heat and simmer gently, stirring now and then with a sturdy wooden spoon, until the grains are completely tender. It will take from 20 to 45 minutes, depending on the size of the grain and its age. Add more hot water, a ¼-cup at a time, if the polenta becomes too thick; it should be thin enough to fall from a spoon. When the polenta is done, stir in half the mustard paste, half the butter and the cheese. Taste, correct for salt, season with several turns of black pepper and pour into a large shallow serving dish. Set in a warm (200 degrees) oven.

When the polenta is nearly done, put the sausages into a heavy sauté pan set over medium-high heat, add the wine, cover and simmer for about 5 minutes. Uncover and simmer until the wine completely evaporates.

Continue to cook the sausages, rolling them frequently, until they are evenly browned. Arrange the sausages on top of the polenta.

Return the pan to the heat, add the remaining butter and quickly sauté the apples, turning once, until just tender. Season with salt and pepper and add to the platter with the polenta and sausages.

Return the pan to the heat, add about ½ cup water and the remaining mustard paste, stir in the mustard greens, cover and cook until wilted, about 4 to 5 minutes. Turn the greens to coat them evenly in the pan drippings, season with salt and pepper. Remove the platter from the oven, mound the greens on top and serve right away.

To drink: If you love California-style Chardonnay, this dish makes a perfect pairing with it. Any Chardonnay will work well, as will Viognier, Pinot Grigio, Vermentino, Albariño and any dry sparkling wine.

Grilled Sausages & Onions
with Assorted Mustards

Serves 8

Grilled sausages, accompanied by onions, mustards, and a salad or two, are a great way to entertain during the summer, as most of the cooking can be done outside. Use whatever mustards and mustard sauces you prefer. In July, when the delicious Santa Rosa Plum is in season, my favorite accompaniment is Plum Mustard Sauce.

2 pounds small onions, preferably torpedo, trimmed

Olive oil

3 pounds assorted sausages such as Cajun, hot-beer, and German

Crusty french rolls, split, or good crusty bread

Commercial mustards of choice

The Devil's Mustard, page 239

Plum Mustard Sauce, page 232

Prepare a fire in a charcoal grill.

Put the onions in a large bowl, add a bit of olive oil, and turn to coat them. Set them on the grill rack, on the side, not directly over the coals. Turn every few minutes and when they are beginning to brown and soften, add the sausages. Continue to turn and cook until the onions are tender and the sausages are cooked through, about 15 to 20 minutes.

While the sausage and onions cook, arrange the other ingredients on a serving table.

Transfer the onions and sausages to a large platter, set them one at a time on a work surface, and cut the sausages in half, crosswise, on the diagonal. Cut the onions in half lengthwise. Return to the platter.

Warm the rolls or bread on the grill and transfer to a plate or basket.

Serving Suggestions: serve with sliced tomatoes dressed with mustard vinaigrette; with All-American Macaroni Salad, page 76, or with Summer Potato Salad, page 79.

Beverage suggestions: Hard cider, beer, sparkling wine, all well chilled.

Skirt Steak Dijon
with Salsa Verde

Serves 4 to 6

Skirt steak is arguably the most delicious cut of beef there is; its flavor and texture are concentrated and intense. It is crucial to not overcook the meat, as it can become quite tough. If you don't care for rare beef, this may not be the cut for you; use hanger steak instead, though it, too, can become tough if cooked beyond medium rare. If you prefer your meat rare, this could become one of your favorite ways to prepare it.

Salsa Verde (see note below)
1¼ pounds beef skirt steak, cut in 4 equal pieces
2 garlic cloves, cut in half
Kosher salt
Black pepper in a mill
2 tablespoons Dijon mustard

First, make the salsa verde and set it aside.

Set the skirt steak on a clean work surface and rub each piece all over with a cut clove of garlic, pressing the garlic juices into the meat as you rub it. Season the steak all over with salt and pepper.

Set a ridged cast iron or similar pan over high heat and, when it is very hot, add the steak. Cook for 90 seconds, turn, and cook for 90 seconds more or a little longer if the meat is particularly thick. Do not overcook or the meat will toughen.

Transfer to a flat platter and brush all over with the mustard. Cover with a domed lid or a sheet of aluminum foil and let rest for 5 minutes.

Cut into ¼-inch thick slices, following the grain, and transfer to individual plates. Add accompaniments (see recommendations below), top the meat with some of the salsa verde, and serve right away.

NOTE

To make a very simple Italian-style salsa verde, chop 1 small bunch of Italian parsley (large stems removed) and put it in a small bowl. Add ½ cup cucumber cut into small dice, 2 minced garlic cloves, 2 trimmed scallions, very thinly sliced, and 2 teaspoons Dijon mustard. Add the juice of ½ lemon, season with kosher salt, pour in ⅓ cup olive oil, and stir. Taste, correct for salt and acid balance, and season with several turns of black pepper. Cover and set aside until ready to use.

Serving Suggestions: Serve atop farro or barley, with wilted spinach alongside; fold into hot soft corn tortillas, with rice alongside. Serve over black beans or other dried shell bean.

Ribeye Steak
with Red Wine Mustard Sauce

Serves 2 to 4

If you love beef, few things are better than a ribeye steak still on the bone. Here, the preparation has much in common with two traditional dishes, Steak au Poivre Rouge and Steak au Poivre Blanc. It is remarkably easy to make. The cooking instructions here are for grass-fed meat; if you are using beef that has been finished on corn, you'll need to lower the heat a bit and lengthen the cooking time by a couple of minutes per side.

2 bone-in grass-fed ribeye steaks, about 1 to 1½ inches thick
Kosher salt
Black pepper in a mill

4 tablespoons coarse-grain mustard
1 cup dry red wine
1 tablespoon butter

Set a cast iron skillet over high heat.

Put the steaks on a clean work surface and season all over with salt and pepper and coat them with the mustard, using about half of it.

When the pan is very hot, add the steaks and cook for 2½ minutes; turn and cook for 2½ minutes to 3 minutes more for rare and 1 minute longer for medium rare. Transfer to a warm plate and cover with a sheet of aluminum foil.

Lower the heat to medium, add the wine, swirl to deglaze the pan, and simmer until the wine is reduced by half or a bit more. Stir in the remaining mustard, taste, and correct for salt and pepper. Remove from the heat, add the butter, and set aside.

Put the steaks on individual plates that have been warmed.

Swirl the pan to incorporate the butter and spoon it over the meat. Add accompaniments and serve right away.

Serving Suggestions: Serve with baked tomatoes, page 195, or wilted spinach and roasted new potatoes.

Beverage Suggestions: This meal calls for a suave red wine, such as pinot noir, Côtes du Rhône or malbec.

Beef Tongue in Mustard Vinegar Sauce
with Roasted Garlic & Saffron-Mustard Cream

Serves 6

A classic recipe from France, beef tongue in a mustardy sauce is delicious and, I am happy to say, enjoying a resurgence of interest, as the current butchery renaissance encourage people to enjoy the entire animal, not just the so-called pretty parts.

1 beef tongue, preferably grass-fed, about 4 to 5 pounds, rinsed and patted dry
Kosher salt
Black pepper in a mill
4 cups chicken or beef stock, hot
1 cup red wine vinegar
2 bay leaves

1 yellow onion, quartered
3 tablespoons roasted-garlic puree, see note page 254
⅓ cup Dijon mustard
3 tablespoons chopped fresh Italian parsley
Saffron-Mustard Cream, optional, page 221

Set the tongue on a clean work surface, season all over with salt and pepper, and set it into a large pot. Add the stock and ¾ cup of the vinegar, along with enough water to cover the tongue completely. Set over medium-high heat, bring to a boil and then reduce the heat to low. Simmer gently until the meat is very tender, about 2½ to 3 hours. Remove from the heat and let cool in the poaching liquid.

While the tongue is still warm, pull off its skin. Cut the tongue into ⅜-inch diagonal slices and arrange them in an oven proof dish, overlapping them slightly.

Preheat the oven to 350 degrees. Strain the cooking liquid into a clean saucepan, add the remaining vinegar, set over high heat, and boil until it is reduced to a scant 2 cups. Whisk in the roasted garlic puree and the mustard, taste, and correct for salt and pepper. Pour the sauce over the tongue, set in the oven, and bake for 20 minutes.

Garnish with parsley and serve right away, with the Saffron-Mustard Cream alongside, if you like.

Beef Tongue
with Mustard Cream, Radishes & Watercress

Serves 3 to 4

What is the point of including two or even three recipes for tongue in a cookbook, many editors have asked me. One even deleted two recipes from a book after the final edit. I didn't find out until an interviewer at a newspaper asked me to name my favorite recipes, which happened to be those for tongue. She looked puzzled, we turned to the book's index, and found them missing.

The point is, I tell anyone who questions, that one recipe for tongue would stand out as an anomaly and would likely scare off anyone unfamiliar with it. Two or more, especially if they are fairly simple and sound, on the page, delicious, will be inviting and encouraging. I developed this one, the third recipe for tongue in this book, to serve with sauvignon blanc or other dry white wine instead of the more traditional pinot noir.

1 beef tongue, preferably grass-fed, about 3 pounds
Kosher salt
Black pepper in a mill
1 large onion, peeled and cut into ¼-inch rounds
6 garlic cloves, crushed
2 bay leaves
4 cups beef or chicken stock, hot
Boiling water

¾ cup white wine vinegar
¾ cup Mustard Cream, page 221
½ lemon, in wedges
8 to 10 radishes, preferably breakfast radishes, trimmed and cut into thin lengthwise slices
2 big handfuls watercress (not hydroponic), rinsed and dried
Good hearth bread, hot

If you have a slow cooker, use it to prepare the tongue (if you do not have a slow cooker, cook on top of the stove as described in the recipe for Beef Tongue in Basic Mustard Vinaigrette, page 226). To do so, rinse the tongue under cooling running water, pat dry, set on a work surface, and season all over with salt and pepper. Let rest a few minutes.

Spread the onion and garlic over the bottom of the cooker and add the bay leaves.

Set the tongue on top, add the stock, the vinegar, and enough boiling water to cover the meat. Cook on high for 1 hour; set the heat on low and cook for 6 hours or overnight. Let it cool in the stock.

While the tongue is still warm, use tongs to transfer it to a work surface and let cool until it is easy to handle but still warm. Peel off the skin, which should pull away easily.

Cut the tongue into ¼- to ⅜-inch thick diagonal slices and arrange on a platter, leaving room for the other ingredients. Set aside briefly.

Drizzle a little of the cream over the sliced tongue. Set the radishes and watercress alongside and grind a little black pepper over everything. Serve immediately, with the hot bread and remaining mustard cream alongside.

Grilled Ribeye Steak
with Fennel, Red Onions, Cucumbers & Horseradish-Mustard Sauce

Serves 4 as a main course, or 8 as a first course

The best part of this dish is the way the juices of the meat mingle with the flavors of horseradish, mustard, and lemon. The bright crispness of the vegetables forms a very pleasant contrasting texture as well.

1 large or two small fennel
    bulbs, very thinly sliced
1 red onion, very thinly
    sliced
1 cucumber, peeled and very
    thinly sliced
1 pound ribeye or market steak,
    boneless
Kosher salt
Black pepper in a mill

1 tablespoon extra virgin olive oil
Juice of ½ lemon
½ cup sour cream
3 tablespoons Dijon mustard
1 tablespoon prepared creamy
    horseradish
3 tablespoons half-and-half
Japanese red mustard or other crisp
    greens

Put the fennel, onion, and cucumber into a medium bowl, toss gently, cover, and refrigerate.

Prepare a charcoal fire in an outdoor grill or preheat an oven broiler. Season the steak all over with salt and pepper and grill or broil for about 4 minutes, turn, and cook about 4 minutes more or a bit longer for medium rare meat. Transfer to a warm plate, cover with a sheet of aluminum foil, and let rest for 5 minutes.

Working quickly, drizzle the olive oil and lemon juice over the vegetables, season with salt and pepper, and divide among individual plates. Put the sour cream, mustard, and horseradish into a small squeeze bottle, add the half-and-half, and shake well. Set aside briefly.

Cut the steak into thin slices, cutting against the grain, and set the slices on top of the vegetables. Squeeze mustard sauce over each portion, garnish with greens, and serve right away.

                                                 A Mustard Cookbook

Honey-Mustard Steak
with Basmati Rice

Serves 4

In a mustard cookbook. it would be unthinkable not to offer several beef recipes, beef having been a happy companion since early history. When I wrote the first edition of this book, many people, myself included, were cutting back on beef, in part because of environmental considerations and in part because of health concerns. Twenty years later, we have much better beef, raised humanely on grass and pasture and not treated with hormones or antibiotics. We also know that beef, especially its fat, contains many essential nutrients we get nowhere else. If you enjoy beef, know its source to be certain you're getting the very best possible.

1 cup All-Purpose Mustard Sauce (page 229)
⅓ cup Honey-Ginger Mustard (page 242)
2 ribeye or market steaks, 8 to 12 ounces each
1 cup basmati rice rinsed
2 tablespoons extra virgin olive oil
2 tablespoons finely minced red onion

2 teaspoons yellow mustard seeds
¼ cup Zante currants
2 tablespoons diced candied lemon peel
2 tablespoons candied orange peel
Salt and freshly ground black pepper
Four fresh mint sprigs

Mix together the mustard sauce and Honey-Ginger Mustard. Coat the steaks with a generous amount of the mixture and let them rest in a nonreactive container for at least two hours in the refrigerator. Reserve the remaining sauce. Thirty minutes before serving, cook the rice according to package directions. Preheat a charcoal grill or an oven broiler.

Heat the olive oil in a sauté pan over medium heat and sauté the onions until soft. Add the mustard seeds and sauté for 2 minutes. Add the currants, lemon peel, and orange peel and toss the ingredients together to heat through. Remove from the heat and add 3 tablespoons of the reserved sauce. Toss the ingredients with the cooked rice and set aside; keep the mixture warm.

Brush most of the marinade off the steaks and grill or broil them until rare or medium rare, 4 to 5 minutes per side.

Working quickly, divide the rice among individual plates. Cut the steaks into thin slices, cutting against the grain, and set slices atop the rice. Add a spoonful of the remaining sauce, garnish with mint and serve right away.

Beef Tenderloin
with Mustard Butter & Roasted Shallot
& Red Wine Sauce

Serves 6 to 8

Although mustard, plain and unadorned, is a wonderful—perhaps the ideal—condiment for beef, special occasions sometimes call for a more elegant dish with more complex preparation. A finely honed sauce served with a well-cooked beef tenderloin is a perfect dish for such an occasion. In this version, the mustard plays a more subtle role than it generally does when used as a condiment.

1 beef tenderloin (head fillet), about
    3 pounds
Kosher salt
Black pepper in a mill
4 large shallots, unpeeled
olive oil
6 cups beef, veal, or duck stock
2 cups full-bodied red wine such as
    Zinfandel or Cabernet Sauvignon

Bouquet garni of fresh oregano,
    thyme, and Italian parsley sprigs
1 tablespoon Dijon mustard
1 tablespoon butter
¼ cup Mustard Butter, page 220
6 to 8 fresh Italian parsley sprigs

Trim the tenderloin, removing the silver skin and any excess fat and saving all bits of meat that you cut off. Season the tenderloin with salt and pepper. You can prepare the tenderloin in advance, but be sure to remove it from the refrigerator 30 minutes before cooking time.

Preheat the oven to 325 degrees.

Rub the shallots all over with olive oil, season with salt and pepper, set in a small baking dish, and cook for about 40 minutes, until completely tender. Remove from the oven and let cool. When they are cool enough to handle, remove the skins and puree the soft interiors in a blender or food processor, adding a little of the stock if necessary; season with salt and pepper and set the puree aside.

Increase the oven temperature to 450 degrees. Brown the beef trimmings (you'll need about ¼ pound) over high heat in a heavy skillet with a little olive oil. When the meat is well browned on all sides, add ½ cup of the stock, deglaze the pan, and simmer until the stock is reduced to a glaze. Repeat, using ½ cup stock at a time, until you have used 4 cups. Do not reduce the final addition of stock all the way to a glaze, but only by half. Strain the essence into a heavy saucepan and set aside.

Put the red wine and bouquet garni in a heavy saucepan over medium heat and reduce by three fourths, until about ½ cup remains. Strain the reduced wine into the stock essence. Put the beef tenderloin on a rack in a roasting pan and roast in the preheated oven. After 10 minutes, reduce the heat to 375°F and cook the tenderloin approximately 25 minutes, or until it reaches an internal temperature of 120°F for rare beef. Cook an additional 10 to 15 minutes, or to an internal temperature of 135°F for medium-rare. Remove the tenderloin from the oven and let rest for 5 minutes. To complete the sauce, stir 2 tablespoons of the pureed shallots into the wine-stock essence mixture. Add the remaining 2 cups stock and reduce the mixture by one third. Add the Dijon mustard and salt and pepper to taste. Taste the mixture again, adding more roasted shallot puree, more mustard, and additional salt and pepper for balance. Whisk in the butter.

To serve, slice the meat ¼-inch thick, cutting across the grain. Pour a ladle of sauce on warmed plates and set the beef on top, fanning out the slices. Top the meat with a dollop of mustard butter, garnish with a sprig of parsley, add accompaniments, and serve right away.

Serving Suggestions: with braised mustard greens and gratin of potatoes, of potatoes and sweet potatoes, or of potatoes and onions.

Vegetables

Nothing could be easier than adding a bit of mustard to a vegetable dish: Toss steamed green beans with a nubbin of mustard butter, drizzled mustard vinaigrette over roasted asparagus, serve tangy mustard cream with roasted Brussels sprouts. The limits are simply your personal preferences and your imagination.

In this chapter, I feature mustard in all its roles, using seeds as a spice, prepared mustards as a condiment and mustard greens as a vegetable.

Baked Tomatoes with Mustard Butter & Mustard Breadcrumbs
Braised Mustard Greens
Cabbage & Celery with Mustard Seeds & Fresh Sage
English Peas with Mustard Butter
Spicy Glazed Carrots
Julienned Carrots with Lemon-Mustard Dressing
Oven-Roasted New Potatoes with Mustard Butter
Baked Sweet Potatoes with Honey-Pepper Mustard & Butter
Gratin of Potatoes
Gratin of Potatoes & Sweet Potatoes
Gratin of Potatoes & Onions
Pappardelle with Melted Leeks, Mustard, & Crème Fraîche

Baked Tomatoes
with Mustard Butter & Mustard Breadcrumbs

Serves 6

Baked tomatoes topped with olive oil, garlic, and breadcrumbs are a classic dish from the South of France, so much so that they are called Tomatoes Provençal. Here, they are baked with mustard butter and mustard breadcrumbs for a version that could be called Tomatoes Bourgogne, in honor of the home of Dijon mustard.

6 medium firm-ripe tomatoes
6¼-inch rounds of Mustard Butter, page 220
6 tablespoons Mustard Breadcrumbs

Preheat the oven to 375 degrees.

Cut a slice off the stem ends of the tomatoes just above the shoulder (where the tomato begins to widen). Carefully pierce the tomatoes with a fork, pointing the tines down directly into the flesh and being careful not to puncture the skin.

Set the tomatoes in a baking dish, press a round of mustard butter on top of each one, and sprinkle breadcrumbs on top. Set on the middle rack of the oven and cook until the tomatoes are soft and the breadcrumbs are lightly browned, about 25 minutes.

Remove from the heat, let rest for 5 minutes, and serve hot.

Serving Suggestions: with simple pastas; with Steak in Red Wine Mustard Sauce, page 258; with Chicken Dijonnaise; with any roasted meat or poultry; alongside creamy polenta.

Braised Mustard Greens

Serves 4

Simple braised greens make a wonderful accompaniment to almost any meal. To highlight these greens' slightly mustardy flavor, use mustard butter. If you've never cared for braised greens or have family members who don't care for them, add a tablespoon or two of bacon fat to the butter and top them with crumbled bacon instead of lemon zest. You'll win converts, I promise.

2 tablespoons Mustard Butter, page 220, or plain butter
1 bunch of fresh mustard greens, trimmed and sliced or chopped
Crushed red pepper flakes
Kosher salt
Zest of 1 lemon
Lemon wedges or apple cider vinegar

Put the butter into a heavy sauté pan set over medium heat and, when it is melted, add the greens. Turn to coat them in butter, cover, and cook gently until wilted, about 10 minutes.

Uncover, check for tenderness, sprinkle to taste with pepper flakes, season with salt, add the lemon zest, and toss. Transfer to a serving dish, garnish with lemon wedges, and serve right away. If using vinegar instead of lemon wedges, pour some into a small bottle and serve alongside.

Cabbage & Celery
with Mustard Seeds & Fresh Sage

Serves 6 to 8

Sage evokes the winter holidays, especially Thanksgiving, like no other herb and it is best when it is fresh. This dish is a perfect accompaniment to any fall feast, whether a traditional holiday meal or something different, such as porchetta, roasted leg of lamb, and even braised chuck roast, all of which have become popular for Thanksgiving in the last several years.

1 small green cabbage
3 tablespoons Mustard Butter, page 220, or plain butter
2 teaspoons white mustard seeds
1 small yellow onion, trimmed and very thinly sliced

Kosher salt
3 or 4 celery stalks, trimmed and cut into thin diagonal slices
Black pepper in a mill
2 teaspoons minced fresh sage
Sage leaves, for garnish

Trim the cabbage, cut out the core, and cut into very thin ribbons. Set aside.

Put the butter into a deep sauté pan set over medium heat and, when it is melted, add the mustard seeds. Cook for 1 minute. Add the onion, toss, and cook until it wilts, about 5 to 6 minutes. Add the celery, cook 2 minutes more, and season lightly with salt.

Add the cabbage, turn to coat it with butter, and, when it begins to wilt, cover the pan, reduce the heat to low, and simmer until the cabbage is tender, about 10 minutes.

Taste, correct for salt, season with black pepper, and transfer to a serving bowl. Garnish with sage leaves and serve right away.

Variation:
- Omit the celery.

English Peas
with Mustard Butter

Serves 3 to 4

A bowl of quickly cooked English peas slathered in butter is one of spring's purest pleasures. Use mustard butter and it's even better. If you can find mustard flowers, sprinkle a few on top and add a bouquet of them to the table.

Kosher salt
2 tablespoons Mustard Butter, page 220
3 cups fresh English peas, shelled
Black pepper in a mill

Fill a medium saucepan half full with water, add about a tablespoon of salt, and bring to a boil over high heat.

Put the butter into a small serving bowl.

When the water reaches a rolling boil, add the peas and cook for 30 seconds. Drain immediately, shake off excess water, and tip into the bowl with the butter. Toss gently as the butter melts.

Season with several turns of black pepper and serve right away.

Variation:
- Spoon the peas and butter over steamed rice that has been tossed with a bit more mustard butter.

Spicy Glazed Carrots

Serves 6

The best carrots can be found, if not in your own garden, at your local farmers' market. I prefer Nantes variety when I can find them and also love the pale yellow carrots, which are delicate and sweet. Rainbow carrots, typically a mix of pale yellow, orange, and purple, make a dramatic presentation.

I pound small carrots, trimmed and peeled
2 tablespoons butter
2 tablespoons brown sugar
2 tablespoons Dijon or coarse-grain mustard
Kosher salt
Black pepper in a mill
2 tablespoons chopped fresh cilantro or Italian parsley

If the carrots are very small, leave them whole. If not, cut them into thin crosswise pieces.

Put the butter and brown sugar into a heavy saucepan set over medium heat and, when melted, add the carrots. Cook gently until the carrots are just tender, from 4 to 10 minutes, depending on their size.

Remove from the heat, stir in the mustard, season with salt and pepper, and transfer to a serving bowl. Sprinkle the cilantro over the carrots and serve right away.

A Mustard Cookbook

Julienned Carrots
with Lemon-Mustard Dressing

Serves 6

I love carrots, as long as they are not overcooked. In this dish, the carrots are cut into matchsticks, which creates a pleasing sensation on the palate. Their natural sweetness pairs beautifully with mustard. They make an excellent side dish with almost any meat, poultry, or seafood.

1 pound carrots, peeled and cut into small julienne
Juice of 2 lemons
2 tablespoons brown sugar
2 tablespoons coarse-grain mustard
1 teaspoon Dijon mustard
½ cup pure olive oil
Salt and freshly ground black pepper

Cook the carrots in rapidly boiling water until they are just tender. Rinse in cool water and drain.

Mix together the lemon juice, sugar, and mustards. Whisk in the olive oil, taste, and season with salt and pepper.

Toss the carrots with the dressing and serve right away.

Oven-Roasted New Potatoes
with Mustard Butter

Serves 4 to 6 as a side dish

Few things are better than perfect little chunks of roasted potatoes, except, perhaps, little chunks of roasted potatoes tossed with mustard butter.

2 pounds smallest new red potatoes, scrubbed
Kosher salt
4 tablespoons butter
Black pepper in a mill
2 to 3 tablespoons Mustard Butter, page 220
2 tablespoons snipped fresh chives

Put the potatoes into a large saucepan, cover with enough water to cover them by at least 2 inches, and add a generous 2 tablespoons of salt. Cook until they are half done, about 10 minutes. Drain.

Preheat the oven to 325 degrees.

Heat the butter in a heavy roasting pan or cast-iron skillet. Add the potatoes and turn them in the butter to coat them fully. Season generously with black pepper, set on the middle rack of the oven, and cook until very tender, about 30 minutes. Turn the potatoes twice during cooking.

Put the mustard butter into a medium serving bowl.

When the potatoes are fully tender, remove them from the oven and tip them into the bowl with the mustard butter. Toss gently as the butter melts.

Season with salt, sprinkle with chives, and serve right away.

Serving Suggestions: with simple roasted chicken; with roast pork; alongside braised mustard greens.

Baked Sweet Potatoes
with Honey-Pepper Mustard & Butter

Serves 4

Because sweet potatoes are so very sweet, I find they need more than just butter to be part of a meal. Mustard and a lot of black pepper are ideal.

4 small sweet potatoes
4 tablespoons butter or Mustard Butter, page 220
Kosher salt
Black pepper in a mill
6 tablespoons Honey-Pepper Mustard, page 241, or other mustard of choice

Preheat the oven to 400 degrees.

Wash the sweet potatoes and pierce them in several places with a thin knife or a fork.

Place on a nonstick baking sheet or a baking sheet lined with aluminum foil.

Set the baking sheet on the middle rack of the oven and bake for 45 minutes. Turn off the heat and leave the sweet potatoes in the oven as it cools for about 15 to 20 minutes.

Use tongs to transfer the sweet potatoes from the oven to a platter. Split each one, add a tablespoon of butter, and season with salt and several very generous turns of black pepper. Add a dollop of mustard and serve immediately, with the remaining mustard alongside.

Gratin of Potatoes

Serves 6 to 8

A gratin, most often made with potatoes but sometimes with other vegetables, is one of the great contributions France has made to the world of cuisine. They are almost always welcome at the table and are especially good during cold weather.

3 tablespoons butter
4 large potatoes, such as German Butterball, peeled and sliced ⅛ inch thick
Kosher salt
Black pepper in a mill
⅓ cup Dijon mustard
1½ cups heavy cream
1 cup Mustard Breadcrumbs (page 262)

Preheat the oven to 325 degres.

Use a bit of the butter to coat the inside of a 1-quart baking dish (a ceramic soufflé dish is ideal).

Spread a layer of potatoes, overlapping them slightly, and season with salt and pepper. Continue until all the potatoes have been used.

Whisk together the mustard and cream, pour it over the potatoes, and spread the breadcrumbs on top. Add the butter, in little dollops, on top of the breadcrumbs.

Set on the middle rack of the oven and cook until the potatoes are completely tender and the breadcrumbs lightly browned, about 45 minutes.

Remove from the oven, let rest for 10 to 15 minutes, and serve.

Gratin of Potatoes
and Sweet Potatoes

Serves 8 to 10

Sweet potatoes add a lusciousness to potatoes, which in turn add a savory element to sweet potatoes that allows their other flavors to blossom. As you peel and slice the potatoes, drop them into a bowl of cold water so that they do not brown; drain thoroughly and pat dry with a tea towel before building the gratin.

6 tablespoons butter
6 medium Yukon Gold potatoes, peeled and cut into thin (1/8 inch) rounds
3 medium sweet potatoes, peeled and cut into thin (1/8 inch) rounds
Kosher salt
Black pepper in a mill
2 cups (8 ounces) grated Gruyère or similar cheese
3 tablespoons Sage-Shallot Mustard, page 247, or coarse-grain mustard
2 cups heavy cream
1½ cups Mustard Breadcrumbs, page 262

Preheat the oven to 350 degrees.

Coat the inside of a wide shallow baking dish with some of the butter.

Spread a third of the potatoes over the surface of the dish, add a third of the sweet potatoes, season with salt and pepper, and add a third of the cheese. Make two more layers.

Put the mustard and cream into a mixing bowl and whisk until very smooth. Pour over the potatoes. Spread the breadcrumbs on top, dot with the butter, and set on the middle rack of the oven.

Cook until the potatoes are very tender and the breadcrumbs golden brown, about 45 minutes, or a bit longer.

Remove from the oven, let rest about 15 minutes, and serve.

Gratin of Potatoes & Onions

Serves 6 to 8

A classic potato gratin is rich and earthy, a perfect expression of a potato's nature. This one is not better, just different, with a lighter texture and layers of delicate flavor contributed by both the onions and the green peppercorns. I find it especially delicious alongside roasted chicken.

1 clove garlic, crushed
3 tablespoons butter
2 sweet onions, peeled and cut into
    very thin rounds
4 large waxy potatoes, peeled and
    sliced ⅛-inch thick
Kosher salt
Black pepper in a mill

3 tablespoons snipped fresh chives
1½ cups homemade chicken stock or
    duck stock
½ cup heavy cream
⅓ cup Green Peppercorn Mustard,
    page 243
1 cup Mustard Breadcrumbs,
    page 262

Preheat the oven to 350 degrees.

Rub the inside of a 1½-quart baking dish with the garlic and then coat it with a bit of butter.

Add a layer of onions, top it with a layer of potatoes, season with salt and pepper, and sprinkle with chives. Continue until all the onions and potatoes have been used.

Put the stock, cream, and mustard into a mixing bowl, mix well, and pour over the potatoes and onion. Top with the breadcrumbs, scatter dollops of butter on top, and cover the dish tightly with aluminum foil.

Set on the middle rack of the oven and cook for 30 minutes. Remove the aluminum foil and cook until the potatoes are completely tender and the breadcrumbs golden brown, about 15 minutes more.

Remove from the oven, let cool for a few minutes, and serve.

A Mustard Cookbook

Pappardelle
with Melted Leeks, Mustard & Crème Fraîche

Serves 3 to 4

Leeks that are cooked long and slow develop a rich sweetness that I find best when it plays center stage, as it does with this simple pasta. Be sure to clean the leeks thoroughly, as mud and sand can hide in the layers of green.

2 tablespoons olive oil
3 tablespoons butter, preferably local
   organic butter
6 cups thinly sliced leeks
2 tablespoons Dijon mustard
Kosher salt

4 ounces crème fraîche, preferably
   Bellwether Farms
8 ounces dried pappardelle
Black pepper in a mill
2 tablespoons snipped chives

Put the olive oil and butter in a large sauté pan or sauce pan, set over medium-low heat, and when the butter is fully melted, add the leeks, toss, and cook very slowly until the leeks wilt. Season with salt, reduce the heat, and continue to cook until the leeks are very very soft, about 20 or 25 minutes. Do not let them brown.

(This step can be done several days in advance; just refrigerate the melted leeks in a closed container and warm them in a small sauté pan or sauce pan immediately before serving.)

When the leeks are nearly done, fill a large pot half full with water, add a couple of tablespoons of salt and bring to a boil over high heat. When the water reaches a rolling boil, add the pasta and stir gently until the water returns to a boil. Reduce the heat a bit and cook until the pasta is al dente.

Drain the pasta but do not rinse it.

Working quickly, put the pasta into a wide shallow serving bowl that you have warmed by filling it with hot water. With the melted leeks in a small saucepan set over medium-low heat, stir in the mustard and crème fraîche, heat through, season with black pepper, taste, and correct for salt.

Immediately pour the crème fraîche mixture over the pasta and use two forks to gently lift and drop the noodles in several places to allow the sauce to ooze throughout the noodles.

Scatter with chives and serve immediately.

Variations:
- Warm ¾ cup Mustard Breadcrumbs, page 262, and scatter over the pasta immediately before serving.
- Sauté several large wild shrimp in butter, season with salt and pepper, and serve atop the pappardelle after tossing it with the sauce.

Desserts

In ancient Rome, spices, lots of them, were common in every type of food, including desserts. We are seeing a resurgence of this today, with Black Pepper Ice Cream, salted caramels, salted chocolate, chocolate with all manner of spices, and more. I've even seen Mustard Ice Cream which, in all honesty, is pretty good. The recipes in this chapter are those that I think are the most practical and accessible recipes for home cooks.

Spicy Toasted Pecans
A Cheese Board with Mustards and Mostardas
Pots de Crème
Gingerbread

Spicy Toasted Pecans

Makes about 2 cups

This was the hardest recipe in the book to test, especially as a part of a larger dish. These nuts are so good that I'd make them and eat them all within minutes. Yikes! What about chicken with a pecan crust, I'd tell myself, or that great salad with cabbage and goat cheese? Oh, well, if you have any left there are several great ways to use them. If not, enjoy!

1 pound pecans, shelled
2 tablespoons olive oil
¼ cup sugar
1 teaspoon hot mustard flour
   (or Colman's dry mustard)
1 teaspoon ground cinnamon
1 teaspoon ground ginger

1 teaspoon kosher salt
¼ teaspoon ground cloves
¼ teaspoon ground cardamom
¼ teaspoon ground nutmeg
¼ teaspoon ground cumin
Black pepper in a mill

Preheat the oven to 275 degrees.

Spread the pecans over a baking sheet or heavy skillet, set on the middle rack of the oven, and cook until toasty brown, about 25 to 30 minutes. Turn the pecans now and then as they cook.

Meanwhile, put the olive oil, sugar, mustard flour, cinnamon, ginger, salt, cloves, cardamom, nutmeg, and cumin into a small bowl, add several generous turns of black pepper, and stir with a fork until smooth and even.

Remove the nuts from the oven, let cool to room temperature, and tip them into the bowl with the spice mixture. Turn them in the mixture until each one is evenly coated.

Spread the coated nuts on the baking sheet or skillet, increase the oven heat to 325 degrees and toast 20 minutes more, turning once.

Remove from the oven and let cool until easy to handle before using.

To store, place them in an airtight container. They should keep well for a week or two.

A Mustard Cookbook

A Cheese Board
with Mustards and Mostardas

When did Americans rediscover the joy and pleasure of cheese? It was sometime between the mid-1980s, when Laura Chenel, founder of Laura Chenel Chevre, wrote her delightful book American Country Cheese *yet couldn't give away samples, let alone sell books, in New York City, as it was at the height of the country's fat phobia. Since that time, there have been many successful books that focus on both American artisan cheeses and cheeses from around the world. By the time Clark Wolf wrote* American Cheese: The Best Regional, Artisan, and Farmhouse Cheeses, Who Makes Them, and Where to Find Them *(2008), which explores much of the same territory that Chenel's book did, the rush was on. There were cheese shops springing up everywhere. Today, it is rare to find a restaurant, at least one in an urban area, that doesn't include a cheese plate on its dessert menu. A bit of cheese with a sweet condiment such as mostarda has long been my preferred conclusion to a meal, but instead of offering my own favorites here, I asked Doralice Handel, who owns The Cheese Shop in Healdsburg, to make the selections for me. She sells her cheeses by mail order as well as through her sweet little shop; you'll find her contact information in Resources, page 289.*

For a simple meal on, say, a weeknight, all you need is an ounce or so of a single cheese with a spoonful of a favorite condiment for each person. At a dinner party when a large group is lingering around the table, enjoying the last of the evening's beverages and chatting long into the night, put together a cheese board, with each cheese paired with its own condiment, along with some toasted nuts and dried fruit.

These are Doralice's recommendations and pairings. Allow about 2 to 3 ounces of cheese per person and about 2 tablespoons of each condiment. If you prefer, choose just 1 or 2 of these cheeses, add one mustard, one mostarda, toasted cashews, and golden raisins.

3 to 4 ounces goat cheese, such as Two Rock Goat (Sonoma County, California) or Garrotxa (Catalonia), with cider mustard or apple mostarda

3 to 4 ounces Estero Gold (Sonoma County, California) or Piave (Italy), with any mustard or with green tomato mostarda

3 to 4 ounces Manchego (Spain) or Txiki (Basque Country), Dijon mustard or red fruit mostarda

3 to 4 ounces Rogue River Blue, with a dark beer mustard or a black fruit mostarda

3 to 4 ounces Brillat Savarin (Normandy), cherry or plum mostarda or
  honey mustard
3 to 4 ounces San Joaquin Gold (Modesto, California), with cocoa nib
  mustard

If you have a long narrow board of food grade wood, that's a perfect way to
serve these cheeses, setting each one on cheese paper, with its condiment
alongside.

Be sure to arrange the cheeses and let them rise to room temperature
before serving.

Add several small knives and small spoons to the board and set in the
middle of the table so guests may serve themselves.

Alternately, fix individual servings on little boards or small plates,
assembling them before sitting down to dinner and then stashing them out
of the way so that the cheese will rise to room temperature as you eat.

Pots de Crème

These delicate custards have a rich complexity. Although the mustard itself disappears into the flavor of the whole, it is the ingredient that draws all of the other elements together so beautifully.

1 tablespoon hot mustard flour or
    Colman's dry mustard
1⅔ cups milk
1 vanilla bean, split and scraped
3 slices peeled fresh ginger
4 large or 5 medium egg yolks

⅓ cup sugar
1 teaspoon grated orange zest
2 tablespoons fresh squeezed orange
    juice
Boiling water

Put the tablespoon of mustard flour into a small bowl, add just enough water to make a thick paste, and set aside.

Put the milk, vanilla bean, and ginger in a heavy saucepan and bring almost to a boil. Remove from the heat and let it sit, covered, for 30 minutes.

Meanwhile, put the eggs and sugar into a medium mixing bowl and beat with a balloon whisk or other large whisk until thick and pale. Add the orange zest, orange juice, and mustard paste and stir well. Remove from the oven, let cool, and chill for at least 2 hours before serving.

Set the saucepan with the milk over low heat and, when it begins to simmer, slowly pour in the egg yolk mixture, whisking all the while. Remove from the heat, cover, and let rest for 5 minutes.

Preheat the oven to 325 degrees.

Skim off any film or foam that has formed on the surface of the custard and strain it through a fine sieve into a pitcher. Fill eight ½-cup ramekins with the custard and set them in a baking dish that you have lined with wax paper.

Set the baking dish in the oven and carefully pour in enough boiling water to come up half the sides of the ramekins. Bake until the tops are golden brown and the custard set.

Remove from the oven, let cool, and chill for at least 2 hours before serving.

Gingerbread

Makes 1 9-inch square cake

No book about mustard or its history is complete without gingerbread, for which Dijon, France, is also famous. M. F. K. Fisher tells of how the aroma of pain d'épice insinuated itself into every corner of Dijon, including the imaginations of all who smelled it. Although this recipe does not follow the traditional recipes of Dijon, which require rye flour and aging of the initial mixture for as long as several months (or years, she tells us in Serve it Forth), it does call for the addition of mustard flour, which the Dijon recipes also include.

1 tablespoon (for the pan) + ½ cup unsalted butter
½ cup brown sugar, firmly packed
1 egg
1 tablespoon grated fresh ginger
2 teaspoons orange zest, finely grated
2½ cups sifted all purpose flour
1½ teaspoons baking soda
1 tablespoon hot mustard flour (or Colman's dry mustard)

1 teaspoon ground ginger
1 teaspoon ground cinnamon
½ teaspoon salt
½ cup light molasses
½ cup honey (see note, page 174)
½ cup boiling water
½ cup orange juice, preferably fresh

Butter the inside of a 9-inch square pan.

Preheat the oven to 350 degrees.

Put the butter in a small, heavy saucepan, let it melt, pour it into a large mixing bowl, and let cool slightly. Add the sugar, whisk vigorously, add the egg, ginger, and orange zest, and mix again. Set aside.

Put the flour, baking soda, mustard flour, ground ginger, cinnamon, and salt into a medium bowl and use a fork to mix well.

Put the molasses, honey, boiling water, and orange juice into a small bowl and mix well.

Add one third of the dry ingredients to the egg and sugar mixture, followed by one third of the molasses mixture; continue adding, alternating between dry and liquid, until all has been added. Do not overmix.

Pour the gingerbread batter into a 9-inch square pan, set on the middle rack of the oven and cook for about 1 hour, or until the center springs back when lightly touched.

Remove from the oven, let cool for 15 minutes, remove from the pan and set on a cooling rack. Serve warm or at room temperature.

Variation:
- Peel, core, and slice 1 pear and add to the molasses mixture. Continue as the recipe directs. Traditional? No. Delicious? You bet.

Sauces

Many years ago when I was running a little college pub near Sonoma State University in the small town of Cotati, located in the center of Sonoma County, a friend of a friend walked in with a whole salmon he had just caught out of Bodega Bay. California wild Pacific King salmon was at a low ebb at that time, with very little available commercially.

The man, a tiny little guy named Bobby who was full of nervous energy, went into the kitchen and began to cook, while my staff looked on incredulously. No one interrupted him.

He grabbed a tub of mayonnaise and a gallon of ballpark mustard out of the walk-in, put some of each in a bowl, and stirred it together. Before long, he was putting platters of just-grilled salmon on tables, the bowls of sauce alongside, sharing his bounty.

I have rarely ever tasted anything as voluptuous and delicious. The fish was so fresh it tasted like it had jumped straight from the sea to the plate, with a short stay on the grill. The mustard sauce, so simple it was, at the time, laughable, was truly extraordinary.

Most of the recipes in this chapter are a tad more complex, but not a lot, as mustard transforms butter, sour cream, crème fraîche, and yogurt into suave sauces, ready in minutes.

Mustard Butter
Mustard Cream
Mustard Yogurt Sauce
Dijon Hollandaise
New Orleans-Style Remoulade Sauce
Basic Mustard Vinaigrette
Caper-Dijon Dressing
All-Purpose Mustard Sauce
Cranberry Rhubarb Mustard Sauce
Plum Mustard Sauce
Dijon Pear Sauce

Mustard Butter

Makes about ½ cup

Compound butters, as butter combined with other ingredients is correctly called, offer a delicious way to add flavor to many foods, from omelets and scrambled eggs to roasted vegetables, fried fish, steak, and burgers. It is easy to make and keeps well in the freezer.

1 cube (¼ pound) unsalted butter, at
    room temperature
3 tablespoons Dijon mustard
1 shallot, chopped

1 clove garlic, chopped
2 teaspoons chopped fresh Italian parsley
Kosher salt
Black pepper in a mill

Put the butter and mustard into the work bowl of a food processor fitted with its metal blade and pulse a few times. Add the shallot, garlic, and parsley, season with salt and pepper, and pulse several times, until the mixture is smooth.

Set a sheet of wax paper or parchment paper on a clean work surface, turn the butter out onto it, and roll it into a cylinder about 1¼ inches in diameter. Wrap tightly and store in the refrigerator for a day or two or up to three months in the freezer.

To use, slice off ¼-inch rounds as needed and rewrap carefully.

Serving Suggestions: Toss with pasta, with rice, with potatoes; spread onto a grilled cheese sandwich before cooking; with broiled chicken or fish; top halved tomatoes with a thin coin and roast or broil; with baked potatoes.

Variation:
* This butter can be seasoned with whatever herb or herbs you prefer, either with or without the parsley (which helps preserve the color). I use sage in the fall and winter; rosemary in the summer; and, sometimes, chervil and tarragon in the spring. Sometimes I combine parsley, rosemary, and oregano to use with a pork roast. I do not use basil because of its high water content.

Mustard Cream

Makes about 1½ cups

This is one of the simplest and most versatile recipes in the world. It is ready in minutes, flatters a huge a array of foods, and is absolutely delicious.

1¼ cups crème fraîche
¼ cup Dijon mustard
Kosher salt
Black pepper in a mill

Put the crème fraîche and mustard into a small bowl, season lightly with salt and pepper, and stir until smooth. Use right away or cover and refrigerate, covered, for up to 5 days.

Serving Suggestions: As a dip for fresh vegetables or shrimp; in pasta and potato salads; as a topping for soups; with fresh cracked Dungeness crab or stone crab; drizzled over avocados filled with smoked chicken; with grilled fish; with beef carpaccio; with all types of patés; alongside roast beef; on tongue sandwiches.

Variations:

- **Saffron Mustard Cream:** Soak ½ teaspoon saffron threads in 1 teaspoon warm water for 15 minutes. Stir into the mustard cream and let rest for 1 hour; stir again and use right away or store up to 3 days in the refrigerator.

- **Lemon Mustard Cream:** Add the juice of ½ Meyer lemon; adjust for salt.

- **Orange Mustard Cream:** Add 3 tablespoons freshly squeezed orange juice and the grated zest of 1 orange; use with duck and duck paté.

- **Green Peppercorn Mustard Cream:** Use Green Peppercorn Dijon in place of regular Dijon. Lightly crush 2 tablespoons brined green peppercorns and fold into the mustard cream.

- **Rosemary Mustard Cream:** Add 1 tablespoon finely minced rosemary needles, 1 minced garlic clove, and 2 teaspoons fresh lemon juice. Serve with lamb.

- **Chive Mustard Cream:** Add the juice of ½ lemon and 2 tablespoons fresh snipped chives.

- **Cilantro Mustard Cream:** Add the juice of ½ lime, 2 tablespoons finely chopped cilantro, and a small minced serrano.

- **Dill Mustard Cream:** Stir in 2 teaspoons chopped fresh dill, 2 teaspoons dill seed, and 1 teaspoon celery seed.

Mustard Yogurt Sauce

Makes about 1 cup

This simple sauce is bit lighter and a bit more tart, more acidic, than Mustard Cream, page 221. Be sure to taste and adjust for salt and pepper until it suits your palate perfectly. It is versatile and, in a pinch, can even be used as a dip for tortilla chips, especially on a searingly hot day when you don't feel like leaving the house.

¾ cup plain whole milk yogurt
¼ cup mustard of choice
Kosher salt, as needed
Black pepper in a mill

Put the yogurt into a small bowl, add the mustard, and stir well. Taste and season with salt and pepper.

Use right away or keep in the refrigerator, covered, for up to a week.

Serving suggestions: with steamed vegetables, especially broccoli; with roasted vegetables, including cauliflower; as a dip; as a condiment with soups.

Dijon Hollandaise

Makes about ¾ cup

It is traditional to make Hollandaise, one of the great French mother sauces, in a double boiler, using a whisk to incorporate the butter. I find home cooks are often reluctant to make it in this way and so I offer a nearly fool-proof version, made in a blender or food processor. Because mustard functions as an emulsifier as well as a flavoring agent, there is very little risk of this sauce breaking. Just go slow and do not attempt to hold the sauce for too long.

½ cup plus 2 tablespoons butter, melted
3 egg yolks
1 tablespoon extra-forte Dijon mustard

1 tablespoon Champagne vinegar or fresh lemon juice
1 tablespoon hot water
¼ teaspoon kosher salt
Pinch of white pepper

Put the egg yolks, mustard, and vinegar or lemon juice, hot water, salt, and pepper in the work bowl of a blender or food processor fitted with its metal blade.

Process for 30 seconds.

With the machine operating, drizzle in the melted butter very slowly.

Use the sauce immediately or hold for up to 45 minutes by sitting the blender container in a bowl of hot water. You can also hold it in a small, pre-warmed thermos.

The sauce must never reach 180 degrees or it will break.

Serving Suggestions: with grilled wild salmon; with roasted asparagus; with poached eggs over roasted asparagus; with poached eggs in fresh artichoke hearts.

New Orleans-Style Remoulade Sauce

Makes about 2 cups

Inspired by newly available paprika from Spain, I have taken a bit of liberty with this classic Nola condiment. It remains true to its roots and you should feel free to use whatever paprika is at hand.

¾ cup homemade or best-quality commercial mayonnaise
¼ cup sour cream or crème fraîche
3 tablespoons ketchup
2 tablespoons coarse-grain mustard
1 tablespoon Dijon mustard
2 tablespoons Worcestershire sauce
1 tablespoon Tabasco sauce
1 tablespoon white wine vinegar
¼ lemon, chopped
2 tablespoons chopped onion
2 tablespoons chopped green onions
2 tablespoons chopped celery
2 tablespoons chopped fresh Italian parsley
1 tablespoon crushed garlic
Kosher salt
Black pepper in a mill
1 teaspoon sweet Spanish paprika
½ teaspoon hot Spanish paprika

Put the mayonnaise, sour cream or crème fraîche, ketchup, coarse-grain mustard, Dijon mustard, Worcestershire sauce, Tabasco sauce, and vinegar into a medium mixing bowl and whisk until smooth. Set aside briefly.

Put the lemon, onions, celery, parsley and garlic into the work bowl of a food processor fitted with its metal blade. Pulse several times, until ingredients are evenly minced but not pureed.

Add the mixture to the mixing bowl, using a rubber spatula to scrape out every last bit of it.

Season with salt and several turns of black pepper, add the paprikas, and whisk well.

Correct the seasoning, transfer to a serving bowl, cover, and refrigerate until ready to serve.

Basic Mustard Vinaigrette

Makes about 1 cup

Many vinaigrette dressings list mustard—generally flour or Dijon—in their ingredients, using it as one of several flavoring agents where it plays a subtle rather than dominant role. There are other vinaigrettes, mixtures where mustard is the predominant flavor, and those are the ones that I believe deserve the designation mustard vinaigrette and are the ones of which I speak here.

Mustard vinaigrette can be made quickly and simply, just before you are ready to enjoy it. When all your ingredients are readily at hand, the mixture can be whisked together in under a minute.

The variations are countless: Change the type of mustard, the acid—red wine vinegar, white wine vinegar, sherry vinegar, balsamic vinegar, lime juice—the type of oil, and the herbs, spices, and seasonings. Add garlic or omit it, mash anchovies and mix them in. Add honey, capers, or sun-dried tomatoes.

This version is a basic vinaigrette, slightly more complex than a simple mixture of oil, mustard, and acid, and a good backdrop for other flavors. Consider the variations listed at the end of the recipe, or devise your own.

1 teaspoon hot mustard flour or
    Colman's Dry Mustard
1 teaspoon cold water
1 tablespoons Dijon mustard
1 shallot, minced
2 cloves garlic, minced
1 teaspoon finely chopped fresh
    thyme
1 teaspoon finely chopped Italian
    parsley

Black pepper in a mill
Kosher salt
½ teaspoon kosher salt
1 tablespoon Champagne vinegar
2 tablespoons lemon juice, plus more
    to taste
¾ cup extra virgin olive oil, plus
    more to taste

Put the mustard flour into a small bowl, add the water and stir to make a paste. Set aside for 20 minutes.

       A Mustard Cookbook

Put the Dijon mustard, shallot, garlic, thyme, parsley, and several turns of black pepper in a small mixing bowl, season lightly with salt, and stir until well blended.

Mix in the mustard paste and add the vinegar and lemon juice. Slowly whisk in the olive oil.

Taste and correct for salt, pepper, and acid balance.

Serving Suggestions: Over greens, pasta, baked potatoes, roasted asparagus, grilled chicken sandwiches, chicken salads, and as a dip with steamed artichokes.

Variations:

- **Lemon Mustard Vinaigrette:** Omit the vinegar and use all lemon juice.
- **Mustard Anchovy Vinaigrette:** Crush 3 or 4 anchovy fillets in a small bowl, add 3 tablespoons red wine vinegar, and stir well. Use in place of the Champagne vinegar and lemon juice.

Caper-Dijon Dressing

Makes about 1 cup

When you want more acidity, tang, and a flamboyance of salt, this is a great option. It's luscious, easy to make, and full of bright flavors.

1 tablespoon Dijon mustard
2 tablespoon capers, drained
1 tablespoon white wine vinegar
1 tablespoon fresh lemon juice
2 or 3 anchovy fillets, crushed
2 freshly grated ounces Parimigiano–
    Reggiano or similar cheese

2 cloves garlic
¾ cup extra virgin olive oil
2 tablespoons chopped fresh Italian
    parsley
Black pepper in a mill

Put the mustard, capers, vinegar, lemon juice, anchovies, cheese, and garlic into the work bowl of a food processor fitted with its metal blade. Pulse several times.

With the machine operating, slowly drizzle in the olive oil in steady stream.

Taste and correct for acid balance, adding more olive oil if it is too tart or more lemon juice if not tart enough. Add the Italian parsley and several turns of black pepper, pulse once or twice, and transfer to a glass jar or bowl.

Use right away or cover and refrigerate for up to 2 days. Bring to room temperature before using.

All-Purpose Mustard Sauce

Makes about 2 cups

Here is a handy condiment. It is practically indestructible, and keeps well in the refrigerator without any deterioration of flavor. On its own, it retains a great deal of heat, the sort of sinus-cleansing kind that reminds everyone who tries it of the Japanese horseradish called wasabi. It forms an excellent base for a variety of sauces, especially dips for vegetables, seafood, breads, and the like. Simply add 3 or 4 tablespoons of your favorite flavored mustard to ½ cup of the sauce and you have a flavorful dip with plenty of heat.

4 ounces (1 cup) hot mustard flour or Colman's Dry Mustard
¼ cup very cold water
¼ cup apple cider vinegar, medium acid
1 tablespoon kosher salt
¼ cup honey
1 pastured egg, beaten
1 cup extra virgin olive oil

Put the mustard flour into a mixing bowl, add the water, stir to make a paste, and set aside for 20 minutes.

Add the vinegar, salt, and honey and stir well. Add the egg and mix until smooth and thick. Slowly whisk in the olive oil to form a smooth emulsion.

(If you prefer, you can make this in a food processor. To do so, put the mustard paste, vinegar, salt, and honey into the work bowl of a food processor fitted with a metal blade and pulse several times. Add the egg and pulse until thick and smooth. With the motor running, slowly drizzle in the olive oil.)

Taste and correct for salt.

Transfer the mixture to a glass container, cover, and refrigerate until ready to use.

Cranberry Rhubarb Mustard Sauce

Makes about 3 cups

Fruit-based mustard sauces have a long history in western Europe. When I wrote the first edition of this book, there were few commercial ones but now they are everywhere. For my palate, most of them are too sweet and so I continue to make my own. This one is great with turkey during the winter holidays and delicious with duck, too.

½ pound (about 2 cups) cranberries, cleaned, with bruised berries discarded
½ pound rhubarb, peeled and cut into 1-inch pieces
1 cup sugar
½ cup red wine or orange juice
1 teaspoon grated orange zest
2 tablespoons Dijon mustard
Kosher salt
Black pepper in a mill

Put the cranberries, rhubarb, sugar, and red wine or orange juice into a heavy saucepan set over medium-low heat and simmer very gently until the berries have popped and the rhubarb is tender; it will take 20 to 25 minutes. Do not let the mixture scorch.

Remove from the heat and let cool slightly. Puree with an immersion blender or in a food processor until smooth. Press through a sieve into a serving bowl.

Stir in the orange zest and mustard, season with salt and pepper, taste, and correct the seasonings.

Store, covered, in the refrigerator and use within a week.

Serving Suggestions: alongside poultry, especially quail, duck and turkey; with sausages, especially wild boar; with other game.

Plum Mustard Sauce

Makes 1 to 1½ cups

Although this sauce comes from a French tradition that calls for prune plums—the plums that, when dried, are known as prunes—I like to make it with Santa Rosa plums, during their short season. It can also be made with other stone fruit, including peaches and nectarines, and with berries.

1 pound ripe plums, pitted
1 cup delicate red wine (Beaujolais, Côtes du Rhône, or Pinot Noir)
⅓ cup red wine vinegar
⅓ cup sugar
¾ teaspoon quatre épices (see page 280)
1 tablespoon Dijon mustard, plus more to taste
Black pepper in a mill
Kosher salt, if needed

Put the plums into a heavy saucepan and add the wine, vinegar, and sugar. Simmer over medium heat until the plums are very soft, about 15 minutes.

Remove from the heat and let cool for a few minutes.

Use an immersion blender to puree the mixture and pass it through a sieve into a clean saucepan. Add the quatre épices, the mustard, and several turns of black pepper. Simmer over very low heat until the mixture is reduced by about a third. Taste, and if it seems a bit flat or doesn't quite some together, season lightly with salt.

Cool, transfer to a glass container, cover, and refrigerate for up to a week.

Serve warm.

Dijon Pear Sauce

Makes approximately 2 cups

This sauce, guided by the delicate flavor of the pears, is more subtle than the Plum-Mustard Sauce or the Cranberry-Rhubarb Sauce. It is elegant and understated and should be served with dishes that complement its delicacy, like the Gruyère Soufflé, page 130, or with the white meat of poultry. A similar sauce can be made with apricots, peaches, or apples, all fruits that pair nicely with white wine.

4 ripe pears, peeled, cored, and chopped
¾ cup dry white wine
¼ cup white wine vinegar or apple cider vinegar
3 whole cloves
1 cardamom pod, crushed
1 tablespoon Dijon mustard
Pinch of salt
Black pepper in a mill

Put the pears, wine, and vinegar into a saucepan, add the cloves and cardamom, and simmer gently over medium heat until the pears have softened, about 10 minutes.

Use an immersion blender to puree the mixture and pass it through a sieve into a clean saucepan. Set over medium-low heat and simmer until it thickens just a bit. Stir in the mustard, a pinch of salt, and several turns of black pepper. Taste and correct the seasoning.

Cool, transfer to a glass jar, and store in the refrigerate for about 7 days.

Serve chilled or warmed.

Serving Suggestions: with cheeses, especially blue cheese; with Ploughman's Lunch; with roasted poultry, especially chicken; with pork.

Homemade Mustards

Making Mustard At Home

Making mustard in your own kitchen can be quite rewarding. It is fun, relatively easy, and can result in some delicious, inexpensive condiments that will serve you well. It is important to keep in mind, however, that you will be limited in the results you can achieve. For example, it is quite difficult, perhaps impossible, to achieve the texture of a true Dijon mustard in a home kitchen, as we simply do not have the necessary equipment. The very best Dijon mustards go through further grinding after they have been blended, a process that gives many of them such a velvety texture. In setting out to make Dijon-style mustard in your own kitchen, keep this in mind from the start or you will likely be disappointed with the results.

Another difficulty with making mustards at home is lack of access to quality raw materials. Finding good mustard flour is not easy, and the labeling of what we do find is often vague or inaccurate. In most markets, mustard flour is generally labeled as dry mustard, but the type—white or brown, mild or hot—is not always included. For this reason, Colman's dry mustard is a dependable choice. Because it is a mix of both white and brown mustard flours, it provides the full range of flavor and pungency. If you know a wholesale restaurant outlet, you may be able to find products labeled dry mustard, mild, and dry mustard, hot. These generally indicate white mustard and brown mustard, respectively, and will allow you to use the two in the proportions you want. The recipes call for mustard flour by weight, which is how you will be purchasing your mustard. Because most of us measure ingredients by volume, however, the approximate volume measurement is also provided.

A few essential rules will help ensure success.

A simple understanding of the chemistry of mustard is important. Its heat and flavor are due to a chemical reaction that takes place between components in the mustard when they come in contact with oxygen and water. Many recipes call for mixing dry mustard directly with an acid or other liquid, but this inhibits the full blossoming of mustard's flavor and heat. I recommend mixing all dry mustard with enough cold water to make a paste. A warm liquid will make a mustard bitter if it is introduced before the chemical reaction is complete. Next, the mixture should sit for 20 minutes, the amount of time it takes for the chemical reaction to peak. The mustard paste can then be used in any recipe. Although I chill all liquid ingredients before adding them to the mustard paste, it is not absolutely necessary. After completing a homemade mustard recipe, the mustard must be allowed to age. Generally, I prefer two to four weeks of aging on the pantry shelf; in that time the mustard will have mellowed and all the flavors will have blended harmoniously. To preserve this balance, I then refrigerate the mustard. Some recipes recommend aging mustards in the refrigerator, but I find this results in an unbalanced product.

Cold liquids should also be used with mustard seeds so that the same chemical reaction can take place without interference. All seeds must be soaked for several hours before you attempt to grind them in a food processor or blender, although they can be crushed, completely dry, with a mortar and pestle.

Another way to make mustards at home is to begin with a good Dijon mustard and develop your own flavorings and seasonings. Using commercial Dijon mustards has certain advantages. It may not be as viscerally satisfying as starting from scratch, but it allows you to make a flavored mustard that you can use immediately, without aging. I recommend some of my favorite versions here, and it is easy and fairly inexpensive to experiment with your own favorites. Keep in mind that once you introduce anything other than dried spices into mustard, you are probably shortening its shelf life. Fresh herbs—which must be blanched or they will not hold their color—introduce vegetable matter and additional moisture, making your mustard more perishable than it originally was. For this reason, mustards that you flavor yourself should be kept in the refrigerator and used within a week or ten days to ensure maximum flavor.

Chinese-Style Mustard
The Devil's Mustard
Honey Mustard
Honey-Pepper Mustard
Honey-Ginger Mustard
Green Peppercorn Mustard
Sun-Drenched Mustard
Serrano-Cilantro Mustard
Cilantro-Mint Mustard
Sage-Shallot Mustard
Olive Mustard
Three Olive Mustard
Olive Anchovy Mustard
Smoky Hot Mustard
Roasted-Garlic Mustard
Spicy Coarse-Grain Beer Mustard
Dijon-Style Mustard, Version I
Dijon-Style Mustard, Version II
Red Wine Mustard
Raspberry Mustard

Chinese-Style Mustard

Makes about ½ cup

This is the easiest and the most familiar of made-on-the-spot mustard condiments, found in nearly every Chinese restaurant throughout North America. It should always be made fresh, about thirty minutes before serving.

2 ounces (½ cup) hot mustard flour or Colman's Dry Mustard
Cold water

Put the mustard into a glass or ceramic bowl and stir in just enough water to make a thick paste. Let sit for 20 minutes, add water to achieve desired consistency and serve right away.

Best Uses: with egg rolls, spring rolls and salad rolls; with roasted meats, especially pork; on sandwiches when you want a jolt of bright mustardy heat.

The Devil's Mustard

Makes about ½ to ¾ cup

I came up with this mustard nearly by accident and it quickly became a favorite. When I was first testing recipes, I experimented by mixing both mild and hot mustard flour with a variety of liquids, just to see what would happen. I thought I was being frivolous when I mixed some hot mustard flour with nothing but Tabasco sauce, but I actually loved the combination and still do. Be assured, it is hot.

3 ounces (¾ cup) hot mustard flour or Colman's Dry Mustard
2 tablespoons cold water
2 tablespoons Tabasco sauce
2 cloves garlic, pressed
1 teaspoon kosher salt

Put the mustard flour into a small bowl, add the water, stir, and set aside for 20 minutes. To finish, stir in the Tabasco sauce, garlic, and salt.

Serve right away or cover and refrigerate for 2 to 3 days.

Best Uses: with sausages; with any grilled poultry or meat; with meatballs; with meatloaf.

Honey Mustard

Makes about 1 pint

Honey contains spores of the bacterium Clostridium botulinum, which can cause fatal food poisoning in babies and toddlers. It should not be given to children under 18 months of age.

4 ounces (1 cup) hot mustard flour or Colman's Dry Mustard
¼ cup very cold water
½ cup rice wine vinegar
¼ cup honey
2 cloves garlic, pressed
1 teaspoon kosher salt

Put the mustard flour in small bowl, stir in the water, and set aside for 20 minutes.

Stir in the vinegar, honey, garlic, and salt.

Transfer to a glass jar, cap tightly, and store in a cool, dark pantry for 3 weeks before using.

If the mustard is refrigerated after the first use, the flavor will hold up for 3 months.

Best Uses: On chicken sandwiches, roasted pork sandwiches, alongside roasted poultry, in vinaigrettes.

Honey-Pepper Mustard

Makes about ¾ cup

Pepper, honey, and garlic are delicious companions and when mustard joins the trio, flavors soar.

2 ounces (½ cup) hot mustard flour or Colman's Dry Mustard
¼ cup very cold water
2 tablespoon imported sherry vinegar
2 tablespoons honey
3 cloves garlic, pressed
1 tablespoon freshly ground black pepper
1 teaspoon kosher salt

Put the mustard flour into a small bowl, stir in the water, and let sit for 20 minutes. Add the vinegar, honey, garlic, pepper, and salt and store well.

Transfer the mustard to a glass jar, cap tightly, and let rest in a cool, dark pantry for 2 to 3 weeks before using.

Refrigerate after first use.

Best Uses: with chicken; with pork; with roasted root vegetables.

Honey-Ginger Mustard

Makes approximately 1 cup

You can use this suave mustard right away, as it made with commercial Dijon mustard, though I find it is best to let it rest one day before enjoying it.

2 tablespoons hot mustard flour or Colman's Dry Mustard
1 tablespoon very cold water
¾ cup Dijon mustard
5 tablespoons honey
¼ cup candied ginger, very finely chopped
1 teaspoon grated fresh ginger
Kosher salt, if needed.

Put the mustard flour into a bowl and stir in the water to make a paste. Let sit for 20 minutes.

Add the Dijon, honey, candied ginger, and fresh ginger, stir well, taste, and correct for salt, if needed.

Transfer to a glass jar, cover, and store in the refrigerator. Use within a few days.

Best Uses: As a dip; on chicken sandwiches; in vinaigrettes; with spicy sausages.

Green Peppercorn Mustard

Makes about ⅓ cup

I always use PIC Dijon Mustard, available at Kermit Lynch Wine Merchant in Berkeley, when I make flavored mustards. It's perfectly balanced mustard, and inexpensive. You can use Grey Poupon in its place, although you might want to add 1 tablespoon mustard flour (such as Colman's) mixed with 2 teaspoons cold water in give it a little extra heat. This mustard, if refrigerated, will maintain peak flavor for about two weeks.

6 tablespoons Dijon mustard
2 teaspoons crushed dried green peppercorns
1 teaspoon whole dried green peppercorns

Combine the ingredients in a small bowl or glass jar, cover, and refrigerate overnight before using.

Best Uses: with patés and meat terrines; with potted chicken livers; on sandwiches; with meatballs and meatloaf; in vinaigrettes and other dressings.

Sun-Drenched Mustard

Makes about 1 cup

The combination of good Dijon mustard and sun-dried tomatoes is quite intense.

¾ cup Dijon mustard
¼ cup sun-dried tomatoes, packed in oil, drained, and pureed
1 shallot
1 teaspoon fresh oregano leaves, blanched (see note below)
Several fresh Italian parsley sprigs, blanched and large stems removed

Place all ingredients in a food processor and pulse until very smooth. Store, refrigerated, in a glass jar.

Best Uses: on sandwiches of roasted tomatoes and chicken; with grilled chicken and fish; on baked potatoes; with cheese.

NOTE
Blanch fresh herbs by plunging them into a pot of rapidly boiling water for 15 seconds. Transfer them from the boiling water to a bowl of ice water for 15 seconds. Drain the herbs and pat them dry between the folds of a tea towel.

Serrano-Cilantro Mustard

Makes about 1 cup

Here, mustard provides a new dimension to the traditional Mexican combination of serranos and cilantro.

1 teaspoon hot mustard flour (or Colman's Dry Mustard), mixed with 1 teaspoon cold water
1 bunch cilantro, blanched and stems removed (see note on previous page)
¾ cup Dijon mustard
1 serrano, stemmed and minced
2 cloves garlic, pressed
Kosher salt, if needed

After the mustard flour and water have rested for 20 minutes, put the mixture, along with the cilantro, Dijon, serrano, and garlic into the work bowl of a food process and pulse several times, until the mixture is fairly smooth.

Transfer to a jar or glass bowl, taste, and correct for salt as needed.

Cover tightly and refrigerator for up to 3 or 4 days.

Best Uses: with grilled tuna, halibut, wild salmon and other fish; with black beans; with grilled or broiled chicken; with almost any sausage.

Cilantro-Mint Mustard

Makes about ⅔ cup

Because of the fresh herbs, it is best to make this mustard in small amounts that you will use in just a day or two.

2 tablespoons fresh cilantro, blanched and minced
2 tablespoons fresh mint, blanched and minced
1 tablespoon fresh minced Italian parsley
2 cloves garlic, pressed
½ cup Dijon mustard
Juice of ½ lime, plus more to taste
Kosher salt, if needed

Put the cilantro, mint, parsley, and garlic into a bowl, add the mustard, and stir well. Add the lime juice, taste, and correct for acid balance and salt. Transfer to a glass jar or bowl, cover, and store in the refrigerator until ready to use.

Best Uses: As a condiment with seafood, especially grilled tuna, halibut, and wild salmon.

Sage-Shallot Mustard

Makes about ½ cup

Sage is one of the world's most beautiful herbs, with its slender grey-green leaves, evocative, at times, of a cat's tongue. Its earthy flavor is evocative of winter holidays like no other savory food.

3 tablespoons fresh sage leaves, minced
1 shallot, minced
Black pepper in a mill
½ cup Dijon mustard
Kosher salt

Put the sage and shallot into a small bowl, add several turns of black pepper, and fold in the mustard. Taste and correct for salt, if needed. Transfer to a glass jar or bowl, cover, and let rest in the refrigerator for 1 day, during which time the flavor of the sage will infuse the mustard.

Use within 5 to 6 days.

Best Uses: tossed with pan-roasted Brussels sprouts; slathered on turkey sandwiches; with cheeses; with slow-roasted pork (page 170).

Olive Mustard

Makes about 1 cup

Olive mustard is an intensely flavored condiment, perfect for mild seafood that enjoys a jolt of flavor. At the Beard House, when I was the chef for a Clos de Bois Winery dinner, we served it with gravlax made with Pacific halibut and served on a bed of celery root, a dish that is nearly as good, and less work, on its own, without the fish.

18 oil-cured black olives, pitted
1 garlic clove
1 teaspoon fresh thyme leaves
2 teaspoons fresh Italian parsley leaves
1 cup best-quality Dijon mustard, such as Maille or PIC
Black pepper in a mill

Either by hand with a sharp knife or in a food processor, mince the olives and the garlic until very fine. Add the thyme and parsley, mince or pulse, and add the mustard. Mix together thoroughly, add several generous turns of black pepper, and transfer to a small bowl or glass jar. Use immediately, or store in the refrigerator for up to 10 days.

Best Uses: with roasted root vegetables; with gravlax; with steamed or sautéed winter squash.

Three-Olive Mustard

Makes about ¾ cup

There is an enormous variation in the flavors and textures of olives, based on both their variety and how they have been cured. When you combine several, layers of flavor unfold on your palate.

1 tablespoon finely minced pitted California black olives
1 tablespoon finely minced Kalamata olives
1 tablespoon finely minced pitted green olives or Italian-style dried olives
1 clove garlic, finely minced
2 teaspoons fresh thyme leaves
¾ cup Dijon mustard

Put all of the olives into a small bowl, add the garlic and thyme, and fold in the mustard.

Stir well and transfer to a glass jar or bowl. Cover and store in the refrigerator for 4 to 5 days.

Best Uses: On tuna sandwiches; in tuna salads; on toasted bread for bruschetta; on summer tomato sandwiches and sweet onion sandwiches; with grilled vegetables.

Olive-Anchovy Mustard

Makes about ¾ cup

Anchovy lovers will adore this mustard and find all sorts of uses for it. I think it is excellent on sandwiches of grilled eggplant, roasted sweet peppers, and mozzarella cheese. It is also outstanding with boiled new potatoes and red onion and with grilled or roasted vegetables.

2 tablespoons pitted California black olives, minced
1 tablespoon pitted Kalamata olives, minced
2 to 4 anchovy fillets, mashed
1 tablespoon minced fresh Italian parsley
¾ cup Dijon mustard

Put the olives and anchovies into a small bowl, add the parsley, and fold in the mustard. Stir well, transfer to a glass jar or bowl, and store, covered, in the refrigerator for up to a week.

Best Uses: Grilled eggplant sandwiches; roasted sweet pepper sandwiches; mozzarella panini; with roasted vegetables; tossed with boiled potatoes.

Smoky Hot Mustard

Makes about 1 cup

The long, slow heat of chipotle peppers is a real treat. You might try this mustard with the Grilled Tuna with Black Beans, page 144, or as one of several condiments with grilled sausages.

1 tablespoon mustard flour or
    Colman's Dry Mustard
1 teaspoon cold water
2 teaspoons smoked Spanish paprika
2 teaspoons chipotle powder

Kosher salt
Black pepper in a mill
1 tablespoon lemon juice or lime
    juice
¾ cup Dijon mustard

Put the mustard flour into a small glass bowl and stir in the water to make a paste. Set aside for 20 minutes.

Add the paprika, chipotle powder, a few pinches of salt, and several turns of black pepper to the paste. Drizzle the lemon juice on top of the spices and salt and agitate the bowl so that they dissolve. Stir and fold in the mustard.

Taste and correct for salt and acid.

Store in a glass bowl or jar in the refrigerator for up to a week.

Best Uses: With sausages; with grilled tuna served over black beans; on vegetable sandwiches; on hot dogs and carrot dogs;

Roasted-Garlic Mustard

Makes about ¾ cup

As suave as Dijon mustard is, it becomes even more so when you add roasted garlic puree, which softens the heat of the garlic and contributes to its voluptuous texture.

3 tablespoons roasted garlic puree, see Note below
½ cup Dijon mustard
2 teaspoons fresh thyme leaves, minced
Black pepper in a mill
Kosher salt, if needed

Put the roasted garlic and mustard into a small bowl and mix thoroughly. Add the thyme leaves and several turns of black pepper, stir, taste, and correct for salt, if needed.

Best Uses: This tender, delicate mustard makes an elegant accompaniment to roast chicken, pork, and all types of seafood. It is also excellent on good crusty bread, topped with ripe tomatoes and fresh garlic, or on sandwiches of all types.

NOTE

To make roasted garlic puree, clean 2 or 3 heads of raw garlic, leaving the bulb intact but removing any dirt that may cling to the roots and as much of the dry outer skin as will come off easily. Place the bulbs in a small ovenproof dish or pan, add about ½ cup pure olive oil and ¼ cup water, season with salt and pepper, cover, and bake at 325°F for 45 to 60 minutes, until the garlic is the consistency of soft butter. Remove the garlic from the oven and let it cool on absorbent paper. When it is cool enough to be handled easily, set the garlic on a cutting board, remove the root, and use the heel of your hand to press out the garlic pulp. If necessary, squeeze the pulp out clove by clove. Scrape the garlic pulp off the cutting board, place it in a small bowl, and mash it with a fork until it is smooth. A head of garlic will yield approximately 2 tablespoons of puree.

Spicy Coarse-Grain Beer Mustard

Makes about 1 to 1½ pints

This is one of the easiest mustards to make at home from scratch. I find that it rivals all but the very finest commercial coarse-grain mustards.

1 cup dark beer, chilled

½ cup yellow mustard seeds

1½ cups apple cider vinegar, medium acid

1 small yellow onion (preferably sweet), chopped

5 to 6 cloves garlic, minced

1 shallot, chopped

2 ounces (½ cup) hot mustard flour or Colman's Dry Mustard

2 tablespoons cold water

1½ teaspoons kosher salt

2 teaspoons sugar

1 teaspoon grated fresh ginger

½ teaspoon ground allspice

½ teaspoon ground cumin

¼ teaspoon ground cardamom

¼ teaspoon ground cinnamon

¼ teaspoon ground cloves

2 tablespoons candied ginger, minced

Pour the dark beer over the mustard seed and let it sit at least 4 hours or overnight.

Put the vinegar, onion, garlic, and shallot in a heavy, nonreactive saucepan and simmer slowly over medium heat until mixture is reduced by two-thirds. Strain into a clean container, cover, and chill.

Meanwhile, make a paste of the mustard flour and water and let it sit for 20 minutes.

Stir in the chilled vinegar reduction and add the salt, sugar, grated ginger, allspice, cumin, cardamom, cinnamon, and cloves. Add the soaked mustard seed and fold in the candied ginger.

Transfer the mixture to a food processor and pulse until the mustard seeds are partially ground and the mixture is evenly blended. Transfer the mustard to the saucepan and simmer over very low heat until it thickens, 10 to 15 minutes. Cool the mixture, place in a glass jar, cap tightly, and age on a cool, dark shelf for 2 or 3 weeks before using. It will retain its flavor for up to 6 months if refrigerated after the first use.

Best Uses: with Ploughman's Lunch; with Shooter's Sandwich; with almost any sausage; on hot dogs and carrot dogs; on burgers.

Dijon-Style Mustard, Version I

Makes about 2 pints

As this mustard ages, it becomes quite smooth and mellow, although it never approaches the delicate texture of the best commercial mustards. Be sure to read about making mustards at home, page 235, before you begin.

6 ounces (1½ cups) hot mustard flour, such as Colman's Dry Mustard
½ cup cold water
2 cups apple cider vinegar, medium acid
2 cups dry white wine
1 yellow onion, minced
5 large shallots, minced
6 cloves garlic, minced
2 bay leaves
1 large fresh tarragon sprig
1 teaspoon fresh chervil leaves
15 whole black peppercorns
8 whole juniper berries
¼ cup fresh lemon juice, chilled
1 tablespoon kosher salt
1 tablespoon sugar

Make a paste of the mustard flour and water and set it aside. Place the vinegar, wine, onion, shallots, garlic, bay leaves, tarragon, chervil, peppercorns, and juniper berries in a heavy, nonreactive saucepan. Simmer the mixture over medium heat until it is reduced by two-thirds, and then strain it, cover, and chill.

When the vinegar reduction is cold, stir it into the mustard paste, along with the lemon juice, salt, and sugar. Let stand for at least 20 minutes; the mixture will gradually thicken and the mustard will begin to mellow. Simmer over low heat for another 15 minutes. Remove from the heat and let cool. Bottle it, cap tightly, and store on a dark, cool shelf for at least 4 weeks, or for up to 6 weeks, before using. Refrigerate it once you begin using it. Its flavor should hold for up to 6 months.

Dijon-Style Mustard, Version II

Makes about 1 pint

This Dijon-style mustard is somewhat more time consuming than Version I, but it is a good example of how to make a finished mustard from whole seeds. It is best to make it in early spring, when chervil and tarragon are both in season.

½ pound brown mustard seeds

2 cups (1 pint) chilled white verjuice (juice from unripe grapes), plus more as needed

3 cloves garlic, crushed

1 tablespoon whole black peppercorns, slightly crushed by hand

6 whole cloves

1-inch piece of fresh ginger, peeled and chopped

3 tablespoons fresh chervil leaves

1 tablespoon fresh tarragon leaves, chopped

2 bay leaves

1 teaspoon fresh thyme leaves

1-inch piece of cinnamon

½ teaspoon freshly grated nutmeg

2 teaspoons kosher salt

Place all of the ingredients except the salt in a large bowl or jar and cover with a cloth towel. Let the mixture sit for 2 days at room temperature, checking it occasionally to make sure the seeds are completely submerged in the liquid. As the seeds absorb liquid, you may need to add more grape juice.

After 2 days, place the seed mixture in a food processor and grind it as fine as possible. Strain the mixture through a stainless steel sieve, using a pestle to push it through. Strain the mixture a second time through a finer sieve. Store it in 2 tightly capped half-pint jars in a cool dark place for 4 to 6 weeks before using.

Transfer the mustard to the refrigerator once you begin using it. Its flavor should hold for up to 6 months.

Red Wine Mustard

Makes about 1½ pints

Pale pink rather than red, this is a hearty homemade mustard with a rich and complex flavor. Be sure to allow enough time for aging; tasted too quickly, this mustard is rough and unbalanced.

4 ounces (1 cup) hot mustard flour
    or Colman's Dry Mustard
½ cup cold water
1½ cups red wine vinegar, low or
    medium acid
1¼ cups hearty red wine
1 yellow onion, minced
5 large shallots, minced
6 cloves garlic, minced
2 bay leaves

1 large fresh tarragon sprig
1 teaspoon fresh chervil leaves
¼-inch piece cinnamon stick
15 whole black peppercorns
8 whole juniper berries
1 tablespoon kosher salt
1 tablespoon sugar
1 teaspoon freshly ground white
    pepper

Make a paste of the mustard flour and water and set it aside.

Put the vinegar, wine, onion, shallots, garlic, bay leaves, tarragon, chervil, cinnamon stick, peppercorns, and juniper berries into a saucepan set over medium heat and simmer until reduced by two thirds.

Strain the reduced liquid into a clean container, cover, and chill thoroughly.

Put the mustard paste into a small saucepan, stir the cold liquid into the paste, and add the salt, sugar, and white pepper. Set over low heat and simmer very gently for 15 minutes, or until it begins to thicken. Remove from the heat and let cool. Pour into half-pint jars, cap tightly, and store on a cool, dark shelf for 4 to 6 weeks. Refrigerate after the first use. It will retain its flavor for 6 months.

Raspberry Mustard

Makes about ¾ pint

This mustard is similar to the homemade Dijon-style mustards, but slightly sweeter with a pleasing raspberry undertaste.

2 ounces (½ cup) hot mustard flour
    or Colman's Dry Mustard
2 tablespoons very cold water
1 cup raspberry vinegar
½ cup dry white wine
1 yellow onion, chopped
2 shallots, chopped

5 cloves garlic, minced
2 tablespoons fresh lemon juice,
    chilled
2 teaspoons kosher salt
2 teaspoons sugar
½ teaspoon freshly ground white
    pepper

Mix the mustard flour with the water and set it aside.

In a nonreactive saucepan, simmer the vinegar, wine, onion, shallots, and garlic over medium heat until reduced by two-thirds, strain the mixture, cover, and chill. When cold, mix it with the mustard paste, and stir in the lemon juice, salt, sugar, and pepper. Simmer over low heat for 15 minutes. Remove from the heat, let cool, and transfer to glass jars. Cap tightly and store in a cool, dark place for at least 3 weeks before using. After the first use, store in the refrigerator, where its flavor will hold for up to 6 months.

Condiments, Preserves & Pickles

Mustard is itself a condiment, one of the world's most popular condiments, right after salsa and ketchup. Yet it is also an ingredient in other condiments. In India, mustard seeds are used in many cooked chutneys. In Europe and the United States, you'll find mustard seeds in the bottom of nearly every jar of commercial sweet or dill pickles. The American South has its pickled okra, typically munched right out of the jar.

When I wrote the first edition of this book, Mostarda di Cremona, an Italian fruit condiment, was virtually unavailable in this country. It was a rumor, a whisper, a tale brought back from travelers to Italy. All these years later, Italian mostardas are available in American specialty shops and there are many domestic versions, some that resemble the originals and others that more closely resemble jams spiked with mustard flour or mustard seed. My favorite has become one I make myself, using quince from my trees.

Mustard Breadcrumbs

Quince Mostarda

Red Onion Chutney

Rhubarb-Strawberry Chutney with Mustard Seeds

Cranberry Pear Chutney

Mustard Pickle

Bread & Butter Pickles

Pickled Okra for Nicolle

Mustard Breadcrumbs

Makes 3 cups

It is always a good idea to have homemade breadcrumbs alongside and the best way to do this is to save bread that is past its prime for enjoying fresh. You can either wrap it, toss it in the freezer, and make the breadcrumbs later, or you can freeze the breadcrumbs. It is a thrill to realize you have some on hand when you want to make, say, Rack of Lamb Dijonnaise, page 160.

3 tablespoons butter
2 tablespoons Dijon mustard
3 cups bread crumbs, preferably from sourdough hearth bread (see note below)
Kosher salt
Black pepper in a mill

Preheat the oven to 300 degrees.

Put the butter into a large, heavy skillet, set over medium heat, and, when the butter is melted, transfer the skillet to a work surface. Stir in the mustard, add the breadcrumbs, and toss to coat them well. Season with a bit of salt and pepper.

Set the pan on the middle rack of the oven and toast, turning once or twice, until the crumbs are crunchy and lightly browned, about 15 to 20 minutes.

Remove from the oven, cool, and store in a closed container at room temperature until ready to use. They will keep, properly sealed, for about 10 days. You can also put them into a freezer bag, store in the freezer, and use as needed.

NOTE
To make breadcrumbs, cut bread that is at least a day old into 1-inch cubes. Run them through a food processor fitted with a metal blade, a large handful at a time, until reduced to small uniform crumbs.

A Mustard Cookbook

Quince Mostarda

Makes about 6 pints

Of all the recipes I developed for the new edition of this book, none surprised me more than this one. It was quite good when I first made it but it blossomed as it rested in the refrigerator so that when I tasted it after about a month, I was astonished at its deliciousness.

I have one enormous quince tree and three smaller ones that I can see from my kitchen window. As fall approaches, branches heavy with ripening quince reach almost to the ground. Most years, I'm too busy to use all of them myself and so I give them away, including to Laura Hagar Rush of Sonoma Aperitif, who is making delicious wine-infused beverages, one that includes my quince. As I gazed on my beautiful fruit day after day, I understood that I must experiment with a quince mostarda.

Mostarda is an Italian condiment that consists primarily of fruit, often dried, poached in a simple syrup that includes mustard seed, mustard flour, or both. It is really the only mustard dish that comes to us directly from Italy, where there are are many versions, some with whole fruit, other as thick as jam with fruit that has fallen apart, as quince is prone to doing. Honey is sometimes used in place of sugar but I prefer simple syrup when I make quince mostarda, as I like the pristine flavors of the quince to shine through. Vinegar is an essential ingredient in mostarda, at least as important as mustard and arguably more so. You'll find several recipes for it in The Good Cook's Book of Oil & Vinegar.

2 cups simple syrup (recipe follows), plus more to taste
1 cup apple cider vinegar
7 to 8 large European quince, peeled, cored and cut into wedges
Generous pinch of salt
Grated zest of 2 lemons or 2 oranges
2 to 3 tablespoons yellow mustard seed
2 tablespoons hot mustard flour or Colman's dry mustard
2 cups organic raisins

Pour the simply syrup and vinegar into a large saucepan, add the quince, salt, citrus zest, and mustard seed and set over medium heat. When the liquid begins to boil, lower the heat, cover the pan and simmer gently for about 20 minutes, until the quince are tender and have begun to fall apart.

Meanwhile, put the mustard flour into a small bowl, add a tablespoon of water, and stir. Set aside for 20 minutes.

Stir the mustard paste into the quince mixture, add the raisins, and cook about 10 minutes longer.

Remove from the heat and taste; if the mostarda seems too hot, add a bit more simple syrup.

Cool, spoon into glass jars, seal, and store in the refrigerator. The mostarda will keep for several weeks. Flavors improve as it ages.

NOTE

To make simple syrup, put 4 cups of granulated sugar into a heavy saucepan; carefully pour in 2 cups of water but do not stir. Set over high heat, bring to a boil, reduce the heat, and simmer gently until the liquid is completely transparent. Do not overcook. Remove from the heat, cool, pour into a glass jar or jars, cover, refrigerate, and use as needed.

Serving Suggestions: with Ploughman's Lunch; with cheeses; alongside roast pork and roast chicken.

Red Onion Chutney

Makes about 2 cups

This chutney is easy to make in small batches, which many home cooks find less intimidating than large batches. Onions are available year round and so there is no need to preserve the harvest unless you grow your own and have a lot to preserve, in which case feel free to increase this recipe. No matter how many onions you use, however, do not increase the spices by the same amount; instead, use no more than ¾ teaspoon of each so that you don't overwhelm the flavor of the onions.

2 tablespoons olive oil
3 to 4 red onions, peeled, trimmed and cut into ¼-inch thick rounds
¾ cup red wine
Kosher salt
Black pepper in a mill
1 serrano, minced

2 garlic cloves, crushed and minced
1 teaspoon yellow mustard seed
½ teaspoon ground cardamom
¼ teaspoon ground cloves
¼ teaspoon ground cinnamon
½ cup best-quality red wine vinegar
Granulated sugar, if needed

Pour the vinegar into a medium saucepan, set over medium-low heat, and add the onions and wine. Cover the pan and sauté for about 5 to 7 minutes, until the onions have begun to wilt. Lower the heat and cook very gently, turning now and then, until the onions are completely limp and have begun to release their sugar, about 30 to 40 minutes. Turn the onions now and then and do not let them take on any color.

Taste the onions and when they are fairly sweet, season with a little salt and several turns of black pepper. Add the serrano, garlic, mustard seed, cardamom, cloves, cinnamon, and vinegar. Stir and continue to cook until the vinegar and other pan juices have thickened.

When the mixture is very thick, taste it and if it is not quite sweet enough, add a bit of sugar, a teaspoon at a time. Remove from the heat, cool, and store in a glass jar, covered, for several weeks, using as needed.

Serving Suggestions: with any curry; with roasted poultry and roasted or grilled meat; with cheeses as an appetizer or at the end of a meal; on sandwiches.

Rhubarb-Strawberry Chutney
with Mustard Seeds

Makes about 4 pints

Here is a delicate spring chutney, perhaps when both rhubarb and strawberries are in season. It is quite delicate and I find the flavors and textures drop off after a few weeks, so use it up, don't hoard it!

1 pound (4 cups) rhubarb, peeled and
    cut into ½-inch chunks
1½ cups brown sugar, firmly packed
1½ cups apple cider vinegar
2-inch piece of fresh ginger, grated
1 or 2 serranos, slit open

Several whole cloves
1-inch piece of cinnamon stick
3 tablespoons yellow mustard seeds
1 cup Zante currants
4 cups perfect strawberries hulled
    and coarsely chopped

Put the rhubarb, brown sugar, vinegar, ginger, serranos, and spices in a large, nonreactive pot set over low heat. Simmer gently until the rhubarb is very soft, 15 to 20 minutes. Add the currants and strawberries and simmer 5 minutes more. Remove from the heat.

Spoon into hot, sterilized half-pint or pint jars to within ½ inch of the rim and seal the jars. Process in a boiling water bath according to the jar manufacturer's instructions.

Set the hot jars on tea towels to cool, check the seals, label the jars, and store in a cool, dark cupboard for 3 to 4 months. If any jars have not sealed properly, store in the refrigerator and use within a few weeks.

Serve suggestions: with cheeses; with light curries; with roasted chicken; on sandwiches.

Cranberry Pear Chutney

Makes about 8 pints

Cranberries start to appear in local markets sometime in the middle of September and are usually available through the end of November and sometimes into December. This chutney is both beautiful and delicious; it is perfect on holiday tables and makes a great holiday gift, too.

16 cups (8 packages) fresh cranberries, rinsed and sorted to remove soft berries

10 to 12 garlic cloves, minced

2 yellow or white onions, cut into small dice

4 to 5 serranos, stemmed and minced

3-inch piece of fresh ginger, peeled and grated

3 cups currants

2 tablespoons white mustard seeds

2 teaspoons cardamom pods, lightly cracked

2 teaspoons white peppercorns

3 whole cloves

3 allspice berries

1-inch piece of cinnamon stick

4 cups granulated sugar, plus more to taste

3 cups apple cider vinegar or white wine vinegar, plus more as needed

5 firm-ripe pears, cored and minced

Grated zest of 3 oranges

Using a hand-cranked meat grinder or a food processor fitted with the metal blade, chop the cranberries as you would for cranberry relish, working in batches until all the cranberries have been chopped.

Put the cranberries into a large nonreactive pot, add the garlic, onions, serranos, ginger, and currants, and stir. Cut a 6-inch square of cheesecloth, set the mustard seeds, cardamom, peppercorns, cloves, allspice, and cinnamon stick in the center, and tie it tightly with a piece of kitchen twice. Push the spice bag down into the ingredients.

Add 3 cups of the sugar and 2 cups of the vinegar, stir, and set over medium heat. Stir until the mixture begins to boil. Skim off any foam that rises to the surface and cook for about 20 minutes, stirring frequently. Taste and adjust for balance and intensity, adding more sugar and more vinegar to achieve both the proper balance and richness of flavors. Stir in the pears and orange zest and simmer 10 minutes more. Remove from the heat and use tongs to remove and discard the spice bag.

While the chutney cooks, sterilize 8 pint jars or 16 half-pint jars and their lids. Ladle the hot chutney into the hot jars, leaving ¼ to ½ inch head room, and process in boiling water or a canning steamer for 15 minutes or according to manufacturer's instructions.

Set the jars on tea towels to cool, check to be certain all have sealed correctly, label, and store in a cool, dark cupboard for 3 to 4 months. Refrigerate after opening. If any jars have not sealed correctly, store them in the refrigerator.

Mustard Pickle

Makes about 4 quarts

    Homemade vegetable pickles are a real treat, and a great way to use extra garden vegetables. Both the mustard and the honey contribute unique elements to this version, as do the whole garlic cloves and sliced fennel. If you make this once, I guarantee it will become a favorite dish. Vary the specific vegetables according to what is available when you make it.

1 pound small sweet onions, quartered

1 pound small pickling cucumbers, unpeeled, cut into rounds ½-inch thick

1 cup chopped sweet red peppers

1 cup whole garlic cloves, peeled

1 cup baby zucchini, trimmed but left whole

2 cups small cauliflower florets

2 cups diagonally sliced carrots

2 cups fennel, cut into medium julienne

½ cup serranos, cut into rounds

1½ cups kosher salt

½ cup hot mustard flour or Colman's Dry Mustard

2 or 3 tablespoons cold water

5 cups apple cider vinegar, chilled, with more as needed

½ cup all-purpose flour

1 cup honey

1 tablespoon celery seeds

3 tablespoons white mustard seeds

1 tablespoons ground turmeric

1-inch cinnamon stick

1 teaspoon whole cloves

Place all the vegetables in a large, nonreactive container. Sprinkle the salt over them and add enough water to cover completely; let sit overnight at room temperature.

Put the mustard flour into a medium mixing bowl, add 2 or 3 tablespoons cold water and stir to make a paste. Let sit 20 minutes.

Add the flour to the mustard paste, along with the vinegar and whisk until smooth. Add the honey, the celery seeds, mustard seeds, and turmeric and stir well.

Drain the vegetables and transfer the to a large pot. Add the mustard mixture, the cinnamon stick, and the cloves and bring to a boil over medium heat. Stir gently until the liquid turns clear.

Ladle the mixture into hot, sterilized pint jars and top off with more vinegar if needed to cover up to ½ inch from the top of each jar. Add lids and rings and process according to manufacturer's instructions in a boiling water bath.

Transfer to a double layer of tea towels to cool. Check the seals and store in a cool, dark cupboard for up to 1 year. If any jars do not seal, store in the refrigerator and use within a few weeks.

Bread & Butter Pickles

Makes 6 to 8 pints

It can be challenging to make dill pickles, as the trick is keeping them crisp, but Bread and Butter Pickles are a cinch. I typically make a big batch because a small farm near me, Ma and Pa's Garden, owned by Cliff and Joy Silva, grow the best pickling cucumbers I've ever tasted.

5 pounds (about 1 gallon) pickling cucumbers, sliced ⅜-inch thick
3 to 4 yellow onions, peeled, trimmed and cut into ⅜-inch thick lengthwise slices
1½ cups kosher salt
4 cups apple cider vinegar

5 thin slices fresh ginger
3 cups granulated sugar
2 tablespoons black peppercorns
2 tablespoons white mustard seeds
1 tablespoon celery seed
1 tablespoon ground turmeric

Put the cucumbers and onions into a large glass or stainless steel bowl. Sprinkle 1 cup of the salt on top, cover with a sheet of parchment or plastic wrap, and set a plate on top. The plate must be small enough to rest directly on the vegetables. Add a weight and refrigerate overnight.

Drain, rinse in cool water, and drain again, letting the vegetables sit in a strainer or colander until they no longer drip water.

Pour the remaining ½ cup of water, the vinegar, ginger, sugar, peppercorns, mustard seeds, celery seeds, and turmeric into a large saucepan, set over medium heat, and stir gently until the salt and sugar have dissolved.

Reduce the heat to low, add the cucumbers and onions a big handful at a time, stirring gently and quickly. Heat through and transfer to a work surface.

Pack the vegetables into sterilized glass jars, cover with the cooking liquid, and process in a boiling water bath according to manufacturer's instructions.

Remove the jars from the bath, let cool on tea towels, and check the seals. Let the pickles mature for a couple of weeks and use within a few months. If seals are not secure, store the pickles in the refrigerator and use within a few weeks.

Serving Suggestions: with Ploughman's Lunch; with sandwiches; with cheeses; as a snack.

Pickled Okra for Nicolle

Makes 2 pints, easily doubled

This recipe is for my younger daughter, Nicolle, who lives in Mississippi and loves pickled okra, which is easy to make and even easier to eat. Feel free to adapt this recipe to your own preferences, with fewer chilies, less garlic, or more sugar. And if you can find the rare red okra, use it!

1 pound young okra pods
4 small thin fresh hot chilies of
    choice
4 whole garlic cloves, peeled
1 tablespoon yellow mustard seed
2 teaspoons coriander seed

1 teaspoon whole black peppercorns
½ teaspoon cumin seed
2 cups apple cider vinegar
2 tablespoons kosher salt
3 tablespoons granulated sugar

Trim the stems of the okra pods to just ¼ inch. Wash them thoroughly; wash the chilies, trim their stems, and split them lengthwise up to but not through their stem ends; you want them sliced open, not cut in half. Set aside.

Set 2 sterilized pint glass jars on your work surface. Put 2 garlic cloves into both jars and divide the mustard seed, coriander seed, mustard seed, peppercorns, and cumin between them.

Pack the okra into the jars, add the chilies, and set aside.

Pour the apple cider vinegar into a small saucepan, add 1 cup of water, and stir in the salt and sugar. Set over low heat and stir until the salt and sugar are dissolve. Carefully taste the mixture and add more sugar if you prefer sweeter pickles.

Pour the liquid into the jars, leaving about a half inch at the top.

Add the lids and rings, set on the bottom shelf of the refrigerator, and leave for two weeks before enjoying.

Lagniappe

Lazaro, who has a little farm in Sonoma, California, known as The Patch, always tucks an extra tomato in customer bags. Nancy Skall of Middleton Farm of Healdsburg does the same thing, offering a handful of fresh basil to everyone who buys tomatoes.

These offerings are lagniappes, a little something extra typically offered by a merchant to a customer. It is a term I associate with the American South, especially New Orleans and southern Louisiana, where people are so hospitable to strangers that they make me want to stay forever. And so, this short and sweet chapter is my lagniappe to you, dear reader. I thank you for making it this far in my book and hope you will, at some point, treat yourself to a soak in a mustard bath and give growing mustard sprouts a try.

Growing Mustard Sprouts
Mustard Bath Salts

Growing Mustard Sprouts

Soak 2 or 3 tablespoons of white or brown mustard seeds in water overnight. Wet a tea towel thoroughly with water and wring it out so that it is still fairly wet but not dripping. Fold it and place it in an oblong glass baking dish (9 by 6 inches is ideal). Drain the seeds and spread them over the surface of the towel, between the folds. Keep the seeds in a warm (but not hot) place for 3 or 4 days, misting them regularly with enough water to keep them moist. By the fourth, or possibly the fifth, day, they should be about 1½ inches long and ready to harvest. Refrigerate them in a sealed container and use them within 2 or 3 days.

Mustard Bath Salts

Makes about 4½ to 5 cups

The dark blue round cardboard box with bright yellow lettering is familiar to thousands of people around the world. It is Dr. Singha's Mustard Bath, said to soothe sore muscles, draw out toxins, and facilitate good health. When I wrote the first edition of this book, I bought a box and used it once, eventually tossing out what was left when it began to collapse during a particularly wet winter. It's not that it isn't effective; it can soothe strained muscles and warm cold toes quite well. For me, the problem is the essential oils, wintergreen, peppermint, and eucalyptus. They smell like a sick room to me, like something my grandmother kept around and pulled out when her husband—her fifth husband, I might add—was ailing. I can't abide the aromas.

But there are so many therapeutic essential oils readily available these days, and so I make my own blends. The main recipe shows a favorite combination of scents and several others that I love nearly as much follow. Experiment with your own mixtures, too.

4 cups epsom salts (magnesium sulfate)
1 cup mustard flour (also known as mustard powder)
1 cup dried rose petals, chamomile flowers, thyme flowers, or lavender flowers
½ cup glycerin (available in pharmacies and drug stores)
15 drops sweet orange essential oil
10 drops jasmine essential oil
15 drops black pepper essential oil

Put the epsom salts, mustard flour, and dried flowers into a large mixing bowl and stir with a fork until uniformly combined.

Set the glycerin in a cup on your work surface and add the essential oils. Stir the mixture into the dry mixture and toss gently with a fork until evenly combined. Set aside for 30 minutes or so and stir again.

Pack into jars, seal with plastic lids, and use within 6 to 12 months.

To use, pour 1 cup (or more) into a hot bath, jostle with your hand to dissolve the mixture, and soak in the tub for at least 20 minutes, adding more hot water as needed if the water cools.

Be sure to either dim the lights or light the room with candles.

Step out of the tub, pat yourself dry, and slip into bed immediately, where you will fall effortlessly into a delicious sleep.

Variations:

- Replace the suggested essential oils with any of these trios:
    1) 15 drops ylang ylang; 10 drops grapefruit; 5 drops black pepper;
    2) 10 drops lavender; 10 drops clary sage; 5 drops bergamot;
    3) 10 drops frangipani (plumeria); 10 drops jasmine; 5 drops black pepper;
    4) 15 drops rose; 5 drops black pepper.

PART IV
Appendices

Glossary of Terms
Tasting Notes
Bibliography
Resources

Glossary of Terms

Alba: The scientific name of the group of brassicas that are commonly known as white mustard.

Baton: The wooden handle on the top stone of a mustard quern (q.v.), used for turning the stone, which in turn grinds the mustard seeds into a paste.

Brassica: The scientific name of the genus of plants that includes the mustards.

Cruciferae: The scientific name of the family of plants that includes cabbages, mustards, cresses, horseradish, broccoli, cauliflower, and more. Member plants all have rounded four-petaled flowers that resemble a Maltese cross.

Dry mustard: A generic term that is generally understood to mean mustard flour (q.v.).

Glucoside: A member of a class of vegetable compounds that, in the presence of certain enzymes, releases glucose and another substance; in the case of mustard, this reaction creates its characteristic heat.

Ground Mustard: Ground whole mustard seeds, generally Brassica alba; has a coarse texture and speckled appearance. Not available to retail consumers; the majority is used by the meat industry as a seasoning in processed meats.

Hirta: The alternate scientific name of the group of white mustards more commonly called Brassica alba.

Juncea: The scientific name of the group of brown mustards that includes Asian mustard and most mustards grown for their greens.

Must: Freshly pressed grape or other fruit juice, including seeds and skins, before fermentation.

Mustard flour: Mustard seeds processed to remove the husk and the bran and then ground to produce a fine powder; available to retail consumers and often labeled as "dry mustard" or "dry mustard powder."

Nemotode: A microscopic parasitic worm that infests certain soils; growing mustard can help control them.

Quatre Épices: A classic seasoning traditionally composed of four spices, white pepper, cloves, ginger, and nutmeg, although chefs and spice manufacturers vary both the specific spices and their quantities to suit their personal preferences. Other spices that may be included are coriander, cardamom, allspice, and cinnamon.

Quern: In France, two large rough, heavy stones used to grind mustard seed to a fine paste; the top stone is turned by a wooden handle called a bâton. The quern was replaced by automated machinery in the middle of the nineteenth century.

Sinalbin: A glucoside present in white mustard seed (Brassica birta, Sinapis alba) that disintegrates upon contact with water, precipitating the chemical reaction that produces the mustard's characteristic heat.

Sinapis: The alternate scientific name for white mustard, Sinapis alba, which has been generally abandoned in recent times in favor of Brassica alba. Some languages—Italian, German, and Greek, for example—developed their word for mustard from this Greek root.

Sinigrin: A glucoside present in brown (Brassica juncea) and black (Brassica nigra, Sinapis nigra) mustard seeds that disintegrates upon contact with water, precipitating the chemical reaction that produces the mustard's characteristic heat.

Verjuice: The tart juice of unripe grapes, now available commercially.

Tasting Notes

Dijon & Dijon-Style Mustards

Source Country/State _____ Brand Name _____

Place of Purchase _____ Cost _____

Color/Appearance _____ Aroma _____

Texture _____ Consistency _____ Acidity _____

Taste _____ Balance _____

Finish _____

Overall Opinion _____ Will Purchase Again_____

Source Country/State _____ Brand Name _____

Place of Purchase _____ Cost _____

Color/Appearance _____ Aroma _____

Texture _____ Consistency _____ Acidity _____

Taste _____ Balance _____

Finish _____

Overall Opinion _____ Will Purchase Again_____

Source Country/State _____ Brand Name _____

Place of Purchase _____ Cost _____

Color/Appearance _____ Aroma _____

Texture _____ Consistency _____ Acidity _____

Taste _____ Balance _____

Finish _____

Overall Opinion _____ Will Purchase Again_____

Source Country/State _____ Brand Name _____

Place of Purchase _____ Cost _____

Color/Appearance _____ Aroma _____

Texture _____ Consistency _____ Acidity _____

Taste _____ Balance _____

Finish _____

Overall Opinion _____ Will Purchase Again_____

Source Country/State _____ Brand Name _____

Place of Purchase _____ Cost _____

Color/Appearance _____ Aroma _____

Texture _____ Consistency _____ Acidity _____

Taste _____ Balance _____

Finish _____

Overall Opinion _____ Will Purchase Again_____

Coarse-Grain Mustards

Source Country/State _____ Brand Name _____

Place of Purchase _____ Cost _____

Color/Appearance _____ Aroma _____

Texture _____ Consistency _____ Acidity _____

Taste _____ Balance _____

Finish _____

Overall Opinion _____ Will Purchase Again_____

Source Country/State _____ Brand Name _____

Place of Purchase _____ Cost _____

Color/Appearance _____ Aroma _____

Texture _____ Consistency _____ Acidity _____

Taste _____ Balance _____

Finish _____

Overall Opinion _____ Will Purchase Again_____

Source Country/State _____ Brand Name _____

Place of Purchase _____ Cost _____

Color/Appearance _____ Aroma _____

Texture _____ Consistency _____ Acidity _____

Taste _____ Balance _____

Finish _____

Overall Opinion _____ Will Purchase Again _____

Source Country/State _____ Brand Name _____

Place of Purchase _____ Cost _____

Color/Appearance _____ Aroma _____

Texture _____ Consistency _____ Acidity _____

Taste _____ Balance _____

Finish _____

Overall Opinion _____ Will Purchase Again _____

Source Country/State _____ Brand Name _____

Place of Purchase _____ Cost _____

Color/Appearance _____ Aroma _____

Texture _____ Consistency _____ Acidity _____

Taste _____ Balance _____

Finish _____

Overall Opinion _____ Will Purchase Again _____

Flavored Mustards

Source Country/State _____ Brand Name _____

Place of Purchase _____ Cost _____

Color/Appearance _____ Aroma _____

Texture _____ Consistency _____ Acidity _____

Taste _____ Balance _____

Finish _____

Overall Opinion _____ Will Purchase Again _____

Source Country/State _____ Brand Name _____

Place of Purchase _____ Cost _____

Color/Appearance _____ Aroma _____

Texture _____ Consistency _____ Acidity _____

Taste _____ Balance _____

Finish _____

Overall Opinion _____ Will Purchase Again _____

Source Country/State _____ Brand Name _____

Place of Purchase _____ Cost _____

Color/Appearance _____ Aroma _____

Texture _____ Consistency _____ Acidity _____

Taste _____ Balance _____

Finish _____

Overall Opinion _____ Will Purchase Again _____

Source Country/State _____ Brand Name _____

Place of Purchase _____ Cost _____

Color/Appearance _____ Aroma _____

Texture _____ Consistency _____ Acidity _____

Taste _____ Balance _____

Finish _____

Overall Opinion _____ Will Purchase Again _____

Source Country/State _____ Brand Name _____

Place of Purchase _____ Cost _____

Color/Appearance _____ Aroma _____

Texture _____ Consistency _____ Acidity _____

Taste _____ Balance _____

Finish _____

Overall Opinion _____ Will Purchase Again _____

Bibliography

Antol, Marie Nadine. *The Incredible Secrets of Mustard*. New York: Avery Publishing Group, 1995.

Aresty, Esther B. *The Detectable Past*. New York: Bobbs–Merrill, 1978.

Behr, Edward. *The Artful Eater.* New York: Atlantic Monthly Press,1992.

Brabazon, James. *Dorothy L. Sayers*. New York: Avon Books, 1981.

Brillat-Savarin, Jean Anthelme. *The Physiology of Taste*. Translated by M. F. K. Fisher. New York: Harvest Books, 1978.

Chapman, Robert L., Ph.D., ed. *New Dictionary of American Slang*. New York: Harper and Row, 1986.

Colman, Louis, ed. and trans. *Alexandre Dumas' Dictionary of Cuisine*. London: Spring Books, 1964.

Fisher, M. F. K. *The Art of Eating*. New York: Macmillan, 1990.

Gray, Patience. *Honey from a Weed*. San Francisco: North Point Press, 1990.

Kamman, Madeleine. *In Madeleine's Kitchen*. New York: Atheneum, 1984.

_____. *The Making of a Cook*. New York: Atheneum, 1971.

Man, Rosamond, and Robin Weir. *The Compleat Mustard*. London: Constable and Company, 1988.

McGee, Harold. *On Food and Cooking*. New York: Charles Scribner's Sons, 1984.

_____. *The Curious Cook*. San Francisco: North Point Press, 1990.

Sawyer, Helene. *Gourmet Mustards: How to Make Them and Cook with Them*. Lake Oswego, Ore.: Culinary Arts, 1990.

Plageman, Catherine, and M. F. K. Fisher. *Fine Preserving*. Reading, Mass.: Aris Books/Addison-Wesley, 1986.

Roach, Jill, and Sheldon Greenberg, producers. *Mustard: The Spice of Nations*. Evanston, Ill.: Beacon Films, Inc., 1983.

Root, Waverly. *The Food of France*. New York: Alfred A. Knopf, 1970.

Scully, Virginia. *A Treasury of American Indian Herbs*. New York: Crown Publishers, 1970.

Simetti, Mary Taylor. *Pomp and Sustenance*. New York: Alfred A. Knopf, 1989.

Shields, John. *The Chesapeake Bay Crab Cookbook*. Reading, Mass.: Aris Books/Addison - Wesley, 1990.

Stone, Sally, and Martin Stone. *The Mustard Cookbook*. New York: Avon Books, 1981.

Tannahill, Reay. *Food in History*. New York: Stein and Day, 1973.

Wolfe, Linda. *The Literary Gourmet*. New York: Harmony Books, 1985.

Resources

Grey Poupon Moutarde
32 rue de la Liberté
Dijon, France

Kermit Lynch Wine Merchant
1605 San Pablo Avenue
Berkeley, CA 94702-1317
kermitlynch.com
(510) 524-1524
Domestic purveyor of PIC brand Dijon

La Boutique Maille
32 rue de la Liberté
21000 Dijen, France
Tél. +33 (0)3 80 22 10 02
moutarde@fallot.com

La Moutarderie Fallot
31 rue du Faubourg Bretonnière
21200 Beaune (France)
Tél. +33 (0)3 80 22 10 02
Fax +33 (0)3 80 22 00 84
moutarde@fallot.com

Founded in 1840, La Moutarderie Fallot is the last independently owned family mustard mill in Burgundy. The company is currently run by Marc Désarménien, grandson of founder Edmond Fallot.

Maille New York
185 Columbus Avenue at 68th St.
New York City, 10023
maille.com

In Manhattan's Upper East Side, Maille, one of France's finest and most enduring brands of mustard, quietly opened this little shop, which has both jarred mustards and mustards on tap. Pierette Huttner, America's first and so far only mustard sommelier, is at the helm.

The National Mustard Museum
7477 Hubbard Ave.
Middleton, WI 53562
mustardmuseum.com
(800)438-6878
Open daily, 10 a.m. to 5 p.m.

Seed Savers Exchange
3094 North Winn Rd.
Decorah, IA 52101
seedsavers.org
(563)382-5990

Index

Index

Index

white mustard, 3, 8, 12, 13, 14, 20, 37, 38, 39, 198, 235, 267, 269, 271
white wine, 116, 139, 141, 149, 158, 169, 171, 177, 185, 233, 256
Wilson's of Essex, xix
Wolf, Clark, 213

Yaddo, xiii
yogurt, 69, 223
youtube.com, 99

za'atar, 164, 165
Zante currants, 189, 266
zucchini, 269

Notes

Notes

Notes

Notes

Notes

Notes

Notes

Notes